D0535172

Adventures in Insight

OTHER BOOKS BY KOHN

Feeling Low?
Pathways to Understanding
Reflections
Thoughts Afield
Through the Valley
A Touch of Greatness

BV
4832.2
,K59

Adventures in Insight

by

HAROLD E. KOHN

D. Edmond Hiebert
Collection

ILLUSTRATED BY THE AUTHOR

WILLIAM B. EERDMANS PUBLISHING COMPANY
GRAND RAPIDS, MICHIGAN

WITHDRAWN
HIEBERT LIBRARY
Pacific College - M. B. Seminary
Fresno, Calif. 93702

111648

© Copyright 1967 by Harold E. Kohn
All rights reserved
Printed in the United States of America

For
our near neighbors
and good friends,
OSCAR AND ISABELL,
who have multiplied
the joys of our
"adventures in insight"

ACKNOWLEDGMENTS

It would be a hopeless task to attempt to give adequate credit to the many generous individuals who have encouraged this presentation of essays. There have been too many who have assisted in too many ways. I do wish, however, to give *special* thanks to those who have helped most in making the publication of this book possible —

To Publisher William B. Eerdmans, Jr. and Editors Calvin Bulthuis and Cornelius Lambregtse, who have always been most helpful in my writing efforts, and who are exceptionally gifted in the rare artistry of mixing business with friendship without diluting either;

To Executive Editor S. George Little and his editorial associates of General Features Corporation in New York City, who have edited and distributed throughout the nation and in Canada several of these articles;

To the many editors in the United States and Canada who have carried my weekly column, "Lift for Living," in their newspapers;

To the countless disturbed souls who make their way to the Hidden Brook Foundation consultation room, seeking help, whose needs have brought forth some answers found in these pages;

To my daughter, Carolyn Kohn Minch, and my secretary, Twilla Kayner, who have patiently deciphered my handwriting and typed manuscripts;

To all the unnamed benefactors who bless an author unwittingly — typesetters, printers, dust-jacket designers, bookbinders, postmen and booksellers;

To *you,* kind reader, for without readers who would write a book?

* And very especially *

To my wife, Marian, the best of all companions afield and at home, without whose supporting encouragement and occasional criticism — always insightful, tactful and gentle — nothing worthwhile or lasting would be produced at my desk or drawing board.

Preface

This book was born of an urge to say in the simplest possible way something significant about man's common problems and perplexities, and to tell how answers and the Answer can be found.

For the most part the articles are brief parables based upon some quickly passing moments in nature, observed at the author's woodland study at Hidden Brook in Michigan. The essays are blends of the reflections of a naturalist, the abbreviated sermons of a preacher, and the efforts of a practicing journalist, stated with the informality of a letter to a dear friend.

Worthwhile books are not written on orders of men, but because writers can hardly resist the urge to share with others what they have found to be of value in their own lives. When Carl Sandburg was asked to confirm a rumor that he had received commission from a prominent magazine editor to write another poem about Chicago, he replied, "Ordering a man to write a poem is like commanding a pregnant woman to give birth to a red-headed baby. You can't do it. It's an act of God!" Poets are more aware than most that commissions cannot produce literature.

Although this author has weekly writing deadlines to meet and book publishing agreements to fulfill, he has never written anything worth keeping, let alone worth publishing, merely to discharge a commitment. If the reader finds anything here that meets his need, it is because the author's own need was answered — from Above. And this book is but the author's blessing, passed on to others.

The final test of the worth of a book is not whether the manuscript is accepted by a publisher, or whether the finished and published book meets with critical acclaim and popular acceptance. All of these please an author, and the first is absolutely necessary. But the best test of a book's value is this: does it make a difference for good in the life and conduct of the reader? Does the book stimulate deeper, broader, higher reflection and furnish new insights? Does it illumine some truth that has been overlooked or forgotten? Does it make plain or brighten some hidden beauty, bringing it to the reader's attention? Does it clarify goodness and make goodness attractive? Does it even offer some refreshment and strength to weary spirits and lead to handling life's practical problems more effectively? Some of these things a worthwhile book is sure to do, whether it is a novel, a collection of poetry, a biography, a work in history, philosophy, psychology, the arts, or a volume of informal essays.

So the fate of a book rests in many hands — the author's gifts and skills, of course, but the editor's, publisher's, printer's, and bookseller's, too, and in the reader's hospitality of mind most of all.

Thank you, good reader, for the kind welcome you have extended to this volume now in your hands. It is good to be in your company for awhile.

—HAROLD E. KOHN

Contents

Preface   7

PART 1: SEEING THINGS

1. Seeing Things   11
2. What Gets Your Attention?   14
3. Insulation Deadens Wonder   17

PART 2: THE INWARD LOOK

4. My Soul and Body   21
5. Crookedness   24
6. Rooted in Silence   25
7. No Matter the Weather   28
8. Larger Missiles and Bigger Men   31
9. The Noble Uses of Curiosity   35

PART 3: SEEING OTHERS AS THEY ARE

10. How Can We Handle Human Conflict?   39
11. A Unified Universe   42
12. Christian Love Is Hardy   46
13. Some Cemeteries We Need   49
14. No Matter How Big the Bay   55

PART 4: THE EYES OF FAITH

15. Greater Fruitfulness   57
16. Beyond Appearances   59
17. On Knowing the Names of Things   64
18. Building Lots   67

9

19. See for Yourself   68
20. Can You Look at Life's Darkness and Still Believe in
       Yourself?   71
21. A Few Words to the Brokenhearted   74
22. Singing in a Snowstorm   76

PART 5: TAKE A CLOSER LOOK AT LIFE

23. Almost!   79
24. Clearing Up Foggy Notions   84
25. Before the Curtain Rises   89
26. Abundant Life   93
27. Failure Is a Badge of Man's Greatness   97
28. Something to Grow On   100
29. When Roots Are Intertwined   103
30. Hunt the Hot Spots   108

PART 6: THE UPWARD LOOK

31. A Man Is as Big as the Things That Move Him   113
32. Rest Your Soul in a Patch of Light   117
33. Of Course Miracles Happen!   121
34. The Universe Goes on Its Mighty Way   125
35. A Morning Prayer   127
36. When New Life Comes   128
37. Prayer on an Autumn Day   129
38. When the Waters Are Disturbed   133
39. Communion with the Skies   137
40. Star Bath   140

PART 7: EYES ON THE FUTURE

41. But What Can You Expect?   145
42. On Reaching the Goal   149
43. The Sense of Things Beyond   154
       About the Author   159

PART 1:
SEEING THINGS

1
Seeing Things

EVERY TIME WE EXPRESS AN OPINION ABOUT the world, we disclose something vital about the nature of our souls. We open our mouths to utter a thought about our surroundings and, lo, our spirits are on parade! We look at a new building and exclaim, "How beautiful!" or "How ugly!" Such a verdict may reveal something about the building, but it also unveils our inner standards of judgment, our aesthetic values, our experience with architectural form, our inner prejudices and preferences.

A group of people standing on the rim of the Grand Canyon behold in awed silence the rocky magnificence spread below and beyond them. A young lady elbows her way through the group, takes one indifferent glance at the vast, steep-sloped valley, stifles a yawn, applies some lipstick and powders her nose. Then she abruptly asks, "When do we eat?" That question reveals next to nothing about the scenery and is no criticism of the Grand Canyon. Instead, it pronounces profound judgment upon the woman.

A visitor at an English art gallery grumbled to an attendant that they could not get excited about the masterpieces there. The guide quietly replied, "Mister, these works of art are no longer on trial. The viewers are."

We do not see things as they are; we see things *through what we are*. Jesus taught His disciples, "Blessed are the pure in heart, for they shall see God." The sinner and saint may each have twenty-twenty vision. They may look at the world with similar visual powers. But, although they look alike, they do not see alike. Taken by itself, no event is necessarily a revelation of God, no matter how surprising, inspiring, or even miraculous. Revelation occurs when God's event is accompanied by man's sensitivity, recognition, and appreciation. Divine event plus appreciation equals revelation. God is here in His world. The impure of heart are insensitive to His presence. But "Blessed are the pure of heart, for they shall see God." We see things *through what we are.*

John Burroughs, one of America's greatly beloved naturalists, made a neighborly call one afternoon upon a woman who knew him and his writings well. She was aware of his love for birds and had noticed how often his feathered friends were described in Burroughs' books. As the woman sat on her front porch visiting with the naturalist, she complained, "Why is it, Mr. Burroughs, that you have so many birds at your place, but I don't have any birds at all in my yard?" John Burroughs had just been watching in absorbed fascination all sorts of birds flitting amidst the shrubbery and flying among the trees around the lady's house. He replied, "Madam, you will not see birds in your yard until you have birds in your heart."

Burroughs' remark deftly points to our human situation and to our spiritual condition. We miss seeing God at work in the world because we do not have enough of God in our hearts. We do not see the Christ identified with every human hunger and thirst, with every human ailment, and all loneliness. We miss seeing Him out there in the thronging needs of men because we don't have Him in here — in our hearts.

We shall see God out there beyond us when we have Him here — within us.

D. Edmond Hiebert
Collection

2

What Gets Your Attention?

IN COMPARISON WITH MANY OF OUR ANIMAL neighbors we humans are nearly deaf. Our ears are muffed and our auditory experiences are meager. What you can hear with great effort at five hundred feet your dog can easily hear at the distance of a mile. And the sound that is lost to you amidst the whistling of autumn winds and the rustle of fallen leaves is readily distinguished by the fox and snowshoe hare.

A deer's hearing is extremely acute. One observer, hidden behind a dense evergreen thicket, watched a doe standing in a clearing more than two hundred and twenty feet away. The observer was downwind of the deer. As an experiment the deer watcher began lightly clicking his fingernails behind his back. Instantly the deer became greatly agitated and left the clearing. The sound was foreign to the deer's experience and spelled possible danger to the doe.

Deer probably recognize sounds that belong to their environment — water running through a nearby forest glade, the call notes of thrush and white-throated sparrow, the drumming of ruffed grouse in a clump of spruce. These sounds do not disturb deer or greatly interest them. They *hear* them, but they do not *listen* to them. However, strange noises not only are heard, but they are listened to intently, and they bring all of a deer's other senses into play. When a foreign sound, such as a hunter's stealthy step, reaches a deer's ears, up comes the head. Ears spread wide, better to catch the sound. Eyes peer into the shadows and the nose sifts breezes for a telltale wisp of man-odor. And if the other senses confirm the witness of the ears, the deer bounds off in search of safety. Almost any sound in its environment can reach a deer's ears, but it takes a meaningful one to reach a deer's interest and attention.

There are few clues to our inner nature more revealing than the focus of our attention. Whatever it is that holds our interest suggests the quality of our character and to a large measure determines our conduct. An ancient fable from China tells of a man whose heart was set on becoming rich quickly. Almost every night he dreamed of great heaps of gleaming gold. At last he could contain his desires no longer and arose one morning determined to acquire a fortune that very day. He dressed in his best garments and made his way through the streets to the city market place. Walking boldly to the booth of a dealer in gold, he seized a sack of coins and casually strolled away. Before he had gone far he was arrested, and the puzzled officers asked him, "Why did you rob the gold dealer in the bright light of day, and in the presence of hundreds of people?" The robber answered, "I did not notice it was daylight, and I did not see the people. I saw only the gold."

We see what we most want to see, and our attention governs our behavior. Whatever a person attends to is a clue to what he is. The person whose attention is attracted to and held by pistons, carburetors, cogs, wheels, and levers is mechanically minded. He who intently watches the gestures and manner of speech and the changing facial expressions of his acquaintances and attempts to understand them is something of an analyst of personality. If a person's prime interest in all matters — when an epidemic of illness invades the community, when erection of a public building threatens to increase taxes, when

an election confronts the nation, when the world is threatened with war — is "How will this affect me?" he is marked as a selfish person. The circumference of his interests is himself.

Many years ago an English newspaper printed this bit of gossip about a famous painter and an equally noted writer: "James McNeill Whistler and Oscar Wilde were seen yesterday at Brighton talking, as usual, about themselves." Whistler saw the notice, clipped it from the paper, and sent it to Wilde with a note which said: "I wish these reporters would be more accurate. If you remember, Oscar, we were talking about me." Wilde fired off a telegram in reply, saying: "It is true, Jimmie, we were talking about you, but I was thinking of myself." No matter the topic of conversation, many a man's subject is always himself. Self is the only interest that holds his attention.

Well, to what are you attentive?

Are you as interested in your duties as you are in your rights?

Do you pay more heed to another's successes and good qualities or to his blunders and weaknesses?

Are you more interested in your reputation or in your character, in how you appear or in what you are, in what others think about you or in what God knows about you?

Do you rejoice as heartily over the good elements in your town, schools, and churches as you complain about their faults?

Do you give as much attention to the drudgery of finishing a task as you do to the excitement of starting it?

Do you delight as loudly in pain-free movements as you grumble over movements of ache and discomfort?

Do you care as much about achieving more depth as you do about reaching greater heights?

Do you hasten as fast to have an impurity removed from your heart as you do to have a cinder removed from an eye or fish bone removed from your throat?

Are you as attentive, polite, and gracious to those you live with daily as you are to the stranger you want to impress?

This is a short list and incomplete, but enough self-examination questions are here to make you miserable for the moment, but better at last, if they fill you with discontent and a desire for a change.

God always honors and answers such a desire.

3

Insulation Deadens Wonder

WHY ARE CHILDREN LIKELY TO BE MORE mentally alive than are most adults? Could it be because they have not yet allowed their minds to become overlaid with thick insulation? Their awareness of the world around them has not been deadened by familiarity. Their curiosity has not yet been dulled by too much adult scoffing at childish questioning, and their capacity for wide-eyed wonder is not yet lessened by the busyness with little things that all too soon robs life of its luster.

Watch a boy and his dog walk through the wintry woods. They take time to dawdle and to investigate the sights, sounds, and smells that greet their senses on every hand. They trace a rabbit's tracks across the white silences. They snap to attention at the cracking of a distant twig. They are fully alive and completely enchanted.

And when, at the end of their sauntering, they bound into the house, the lad and his furry friend remain highly impressionable. There follows much exploration of the pots and kettles on the cook stove, and a zestful scenting of their contents. They listen for clues that dinner is ready. They respond with delight to every word or gesture of affection.

Their inner joy finds expression in the boy's excited talk and the dog's glad wagging of his "happy ending."

A little lad and his dog are open to the world. They keenly sense their surroundings, and something of the abundance of

17

life within them makes itself felt on the world around them. Their uninsulated condition makes it possible for a two-way current to flow from the world to them and from them to the world.

Children and their dogs teach us something of what we should be. If it is easy to disappoint them and make them sad, it is just as easy to make them happy. If they are quickly impressed by our harsh scoldings and punishment, they are as instantly responsive to our praise and kindness. This appreciation of the surrounding world, this openness to experience, and this free flow of good between the outside and the inner world are greatly needed by all of us. This kind of childlikeness we must never lose. We become emotionally and spiritually insulated at our own peril.

The spiritually healthy person does not feel less grief, pain, and discouragement than does his fellow man. He feels more, much more. He feels his own, plus that of others around him, because he is not insulated against their feelings by his own self-centeredness. He is open to their anguish. But while the vital person senses more of the world's trouble, he also feels more of the world's joy. His lack of selfish insulation leaves him open to the excitement and glory of another's achievement. He partakes of a neighbor's quiet pride in his home and of a friend's delight in his family and rejoices with a fellow worker who receives a raise in pay or an important promotion. Another's gentle amusement becomes his own, and he shares a smile or a laugh. He joins in another's prayer.

He takes time, refusing to be "too busy" to read the great books and the Good Book, to listen to the finest music, to absorb the glories of nature, to become slowly saturated with enriching friendships, to converse with the Great Companion.

The healthy, sound spirit is like an alert youngster walking in the woods; the boy is in the woods, but the woods is also in the boy. So with the fully alive soul; he is in God's world, but the world of joys and sorrows, the world of man's need and God's power, is in him, too.

We need to strip ourselves of insulation so that we may feel

the electric surge of God's world moving in upon us and
the world might sense the response of our souls to its need.

PART 2:
THE INWARD LOOK

4

My Soul and Body

SOME TIME AGO A CARTOON APPEARED IN A national magazine showing a very little boy attempting to lead a huge Saint Bernard dog on a leash. The dog was perversely protesting and insisted upon trying to drag the boy off in the opposite direction. The lad suddenly braced his feet, turned upon the dog and angrily exclaimed, "Let's get this straight! You are my dog. I'm not your boy!"

Some such sacred stubbornness as the boy showed is needed by all of us. We are often hauled off in some direction we should not go by powers unworthy to be our leaders. Some of these leaders are in politics, some in education, some in religion and some in entertainment, but most often they are *inside us*. The beasts that tug us away from our best course are our selfishness, vagrant wishes, untamed moods, primal passions, fears, hostilities, and all those other inner refusals to be what we ought to be and to do what we know is best. We need the perspective of the lad with the dog, so that the soul will say to every other aspect of our human nature, "Now, let's get this straight. You belong to me and not I to you." Soul is master here. It is the ongoing thing, the lasting reality, and should be in control.

The word "soul" is a rich old word that is heard too seldom

these days except in poetry and religion. Perhaps the reason for its rare use is that it has had so many meanings that we cannot be certain which definition another person has in mind when he is using the word; therefore the word has been dropped from some people's vocabulary for clarity's sake. Primitive people thought of the soul as a shadowy, misty replica of the body, much like breath. It was capable of leaving the body during sleep and returning before a person awakened. This vaporous image of the body survived the body after death. Many Greek philosophers understood the soul to be man's essence, his life, consciousness, and intelligence. Plato believed the soul existed before the body, and Aristotle taught that the body's purpose is to exist for the soul's use.

The biblical use of the word "soul" varies from passage to passage. In the Old Testament it basically means the life principle of the living being, and it has much the same significance as our word "self," being the center of urges, emotions, and purposes. The New Testament word "psyche," often translated "soul," usually means the inner vitality, the life of a person that is hidden within the body but expressed through the body. It is the center of life's vital choices and the place where the destiny-determining decisions are made. Thus does a prosperous man use the word "soul" in the Gospel of Luke (12:15-21). His crops have been abundant and his bins and barns have overflowed with harvest. "And he said, 'I will do this: I will pull down my barns, and build larger ones; and there I will store all my grain and my goods. And I will say to my soul, Soul, you have ample goods laid up for many years; take your ease, eat, drink, be merry!' But God said to him, 'Fool! This night your soul is required of you. . . .' " That man's soul was the essential substance, the decision-making part of the man that determined what would happen to his crops, his barns, his body and his destiny. The soul is that essential selfhood that is intended to lead all other aspects of our lives. We get into trouble when life's other aspects lead the soul, when more crops and more barns lead us away from God, for example.

Long ago, William James of Harvard insisted in his Inger-soll Lectures that the body appears to be more of an instrument than anything else. It is to be used by the mind as a man uses a tool. Observation provides abundant evidence that James was right. When wisely used, the body serves the higher inner na-ture. We use eyes to see with, hands to feel and work with, lips to speak with. We command our feet to "Go there," and, if all is well with us, our feet go where they are told. An ath-lete's sense of the goal drives his body to astonishing lengths, so that long after the body is fatigued from running the miler continues to run. After the body is tired of swimming the com-petitive swimmer swims on. The bone-tired doctor watching over his gravely ill patient denies his body rest, and the body obeys the physician's high intent.

The supreme business of life is to see that the soul is healthy and controlled by the consciousness of God, and that it makes the best uses of the body to advance its high purposes and to fulfill its glorious possibilities. Then our primal pas-sions become the servants of our souls rather than our masters; spirit triumphs over wayward urges of the flesh, holi-ness over sin, trust over fear, love over hostility, hope over discouragement, joy over misery, and eternal life becomes vic-torious over time and death.

One of life's pivotal decisions comes when a soul says to the body, "Let's get this straight. You belong to me, not I to you — and we both belong to God."

5

Crookedness

Brooks become crooked
from taking the path
of least resistance.
So do people.

24

6

Rooted in Silence

THIS HAS BEEN A DAY OF VAST, GRAY QUIET-
ness. Silently the heavy clouds roll over the bay. Soundlessly a lonely herring gull drifts by. The open pools amidst
the ice floes on the lake are still, and the sun-softened masses
of drifting ice touch each other as softly as the brush of velvet
against velvet. This is a suspenseful silence, as if the wet earth
is waiting for some momentous event that is already hours
overdue.

These quiet springtime hours are a part of that creative and
beneficent silence that nature draws about herself while sum-
moning forces that soon show themselves in power: the still-
ness of seeds before they sprout into life; the gravelike hush
of incubating eggs, the soundlessness of sunshine warming the
earth toward fruitfulness; the hidden, quiet years of an unknown greatness maturing in little children, unseen even by
those who know them best.

All the great things have their roots in silence, and life's
most important business is undertaken in quietness.

The French philosopher, physicist, and mathematician Blaise
Pascal once declared that all the world's trouble is due to the
fact that man cannot sit still in a room. He must chatter, flirt,
gamble or hunt for something. Perhaps this is a chief difference between people of inner culture and those without it:
the man of great inner development does not need to live in
a dither of outward activity to distract him from the un-
pleasantness of his inner emptiness.

A small cup, only one-fourth full of water, can be shaken
until it makes a big splash. But hold it still and its near emptiness is revealed. Is this generation's fussy activism a substitute for awareness of what we are and what we ought to be?
Are we keeping busy so that we can avoid self-discovery?

If we want to discover our real inner needs, if we want

to know what we are really like, and if we want God's fullness to replace our emptiness, we must learn to bring a daily halt to our frenzied activity, and to "hold still" for a while. The book of Isaiah says concerning an ancient people, "Their strength is to sit still."

The great matters of life may blossom in activity, but they are rooted in silence.

7

No Matter the Weather

FOR SOME WEEKS NOW THE SHRILL CRIES OF killdeer plovers have haunted the misty lowlands near the lake at sunrise and at sunset; their wind-loving wings have beat the air and their sharp calls have broken the silences of this lakeshore pastel paradise. Killdeer are among the first of our bird neighbors to return from their winter resorting in the South, and their arrival is prophetic of the whirring of countless wings as multitudes of frail but dauntless spirits come trooping into this slowly awakening land.

Now the great river of migration flows northward. From the southern states of our country and from Central and South America, on determined wings the wayfarers come. Some spurn the night and fly only by day. Others scorn the day and fly by night. Many birds, including geese, ducks, and shorebirds, fly at great heights, often more than a mile above the greening land. Others, such as sparrows, warblers, hummingbirds, and vireos, fly just above budded treetops and have been seen by crews of fishing boats off the Florida coast, barely skimming the water as they headed for North America. Herons poke along at twenty miles per hour while some ducks and geese exceed fifty.

Although they may possess a wide variety of traveling habits, there is one thing these air voyagers have in common: a

certain dependability. My nature diary indicates killdeer arrive on the beach year after year with a high degree of prompt-
ness, regardless of the weather. This year's first wild, shrill,
plaintive call was heard, almost to a day, a year later than last
spring's first killdeer cry. The purple martins returned to their
apartment house on a post where our lawn meets the beach on
April 22 this year. The date of their arrival varies little from
spring to spring — no matter the weather. It would appear they
were overly impulsive in their rush northward this spring, for
we have had much cold, wet weather since they came. But
they are undaunted. And along the far edge of the lengthened

days of this damp and frigid spring they fly and emit tiny, bright sparks of song against the darkening sky. And so with song sparrows, wood thrushes, wrens and all the feathered hosts that cascade from warmer climes toward the land of birch and evergreen — they are moved by profound urgency and not by whim; they come here driven by a pressing purpose that beats down fear and conquers fatigue. When the migratory urge (triggered, some ornithologists believe, by changes in duration and intensity of light) commands, the birds obey. They do not wait for ideal conditions. They seek no guarantee of continual fair weather. They will not be discouraged and cancel their spring's migration because of an adverse wind or a frosty night. These travelers have surrendered unconditionally to the inner imperative.

Few secrets of achievement are so important as to have a purpose so worthwhile that one persists in it in all kinds of spiritual weather — through clouds of discouragement and storms of criticism, against winds of opposition, and without regard for threatening consequences. This does not mean that foul weather can be ignored. There is only stupidity in that, not courage. Courage is not ignorance of bad weather but persistence in the face of it. The world's most noble achievers have known as much dismay, regret, and temporary shame at failure as have the quitters, but the victors have subordinated their moods to something they have regarded as far more important than variable feelings.

The ultimate conditions of life — such as love, battle for one's homeland, lofty purpose — are all assailed by adversity. The wayfarer who reaches his goal is one whose dedication is stronger than the storm.

Larger Missiles and Bigger Men

THE INNOCENT SILENCE AND MAJESTIC PEACE of our golden neighbor, the moon, is doomed. Already the Russians and Americans have begun to leave spent space contrivances on the moon and have dumped the initial contributions of man's trash there. Soon, in a few months or years, man will likely visit the orb himself and further clutter the place with his flags of conquest and other paraphernalia of civilization.

If the Russians get there first, no doubt they will leave the place plastered with hammer-and-sickle emblems and with tracts on the communism of Marx, Engels, and Lenin.

If Americans get there first they will likely substantiate their claims to the place by leaving it as Americans leave their picnic sites — strewn with tin cans, pop and beer bottles, gum and candy wrappers and the omnipresent paper napkins. No later explorer could doubt that a typical American had visited the moon!

Building interstellar missiles may be a "must" in these days of scientific advance. But we must not fool ourselves that improving our inventions improves us. Giving a nation space capsules is like presenting a bicycle to a boy. It will not appreciably improve the behavior of the child. It will but spread his behavior over a wider area. A good or bad child can make his goodness or badness felt farther from home. So with a nation and its missiles.

While we have made tremendous progress in our technology, are we much better people than we were fifty years ago? The Russians have advanced astonishingly in scientific research, but they still substitute the threat of brute force for honorable dealings with other nations. Americans enjoy a much higher standard of living than they did one-half century ago. Judged by what we eat and wear, the houses we inhabit, our modes of transportation and communication and the amount of leisure

we delight in, we have progressed immeasurably. But judged by what we *are,* our advancement is at a snail's pace.

Many a man-made thing in our world is getting bigger — bigger rockets, bigger airplanes, bigger ships, bigger buildings, bigger governments, bigger national ·debts. But man's spirit remains about the same size.

The following note was written by an irritated journalist: "Hurry as we may, we are hemmed in by a surging crowd in front and a dense throng of people pressing in from the rear. One man digs his elbow into me, another a pole; one bangs my head with a plant. . . . You can be considered foolish and thoughtless . . . if you go out . . . without your will made." The same writer later complained, "Here you may pay a big rent for a miserable house. Everyone dresses above his means." Do these sound like your problems and your frustrations? They are quotations from the Roman, Juvenal, who lived from A.D. 60 to 140, but they could just as well have come from some twentieth-century writer living in New York, California, or Texas.

Basically, our problems have changed only a little since Juvenal's day. Our greatest difficulties are not with the external symbols of civilization but with the people who make up the "surging crowd," with people who push and make exorbitant charges and live beyond their means. Our chief distresses do not come from modern armament for war but from the suspicions, jealousies, hatreds, and greed that make armament dangerous.

Our progress reminds us of our folly. We are producing bigger rockets and missiles. Now we need to be bigger men and women, bigger of thought and aspiration, bigger in compassion, bigger of heart. For the future of the world will depend less upon the caliber of shells and missiles made for war on earth or exploration of space than upon the caliber of human beings who run our governments, manage our homes and teach our children.

An unlettered woman once declared with mixed penitence and pride, "I ain't what I ought to be; I ain't what I'm going to

33

be; but I'm better than I was." Some such aim should be the aim of all of us, to be better than we were. We cannot afford to be small people in a world of bigger and more powerful governments, bigger weapons, bigger threats to our survival, bigger testings of our characters. These are days for greatness. God needs people who are better than they were yesteryear and yesterday.

So our work is cut out for us — the work of the churches, schools and homes — to produce men to match our missiles.

The Noble Uses of Curiosity

CURIOSITY IS AMONG THE NECESSARY INstincts for any high form of life. Especially those animals that are scantily armed need an abundance of inquisitiveness. It is by their curiosity, mixed with fear, that they survive. Curiosity prompts the rabbit, squirrel, and deer, the ruffed grouse, pheasant, and wild turkey to look intently at everything that moves in their field of vision, to investigate their surroundings with eye, ear, and nose, and to decide whether harm or good lies there. All creatures of a high order possess the spirit of questioning; they are curious.

Curiosity is present to a peculiar degree in human beings and manifests itself in countless ways.

Why is it that nobody who can read is ever effective in cleaning up an attic? Curiosity!

Why is it that if you tell a person there are 281,796,349,973 stars in the heavens he will instantly believe you, but post a sign that says "Wet Paint" on a door or a chair and he must test it and see for himself? Curiosity!

Why is it that the newspaper of the person sitting next to you on the bus is so irresistibly fascinating that you simply must sneak a peek at it over your neighbor's shoulder? Curiosity!

Why is it that the thinner the ice on a pond, the more tempting it is to test it and see if it will bear your weight? Curiosity!

Why is it that the quickest way to get your wife home from a trip out of town is to send her a copy of the local paper with one item clipped out? Curiosity!

Curiosity is a driving force in the worst people and in the best, and examples of the lowest and highest expressions of this urge can be found in every community.

It is present in the meddlers and the trouble makers. A severe, sour-faced, tough-minded woman complained to the county sheriff because several small boys were swimming nude in a stream near her home. She said they could easily be seen from her porch, and the situation was disgraceful. The sheriff must do his duty and put a stop to this degrading practice. So the sheriff came to the site, found the boys and told them they must do their swimming upstream, far from the lady's house.

After a few days the sheriff received another call from the woman who was fretting about the boys and their uncouth swimming in the nude. The sheriff asked, "Haven't they moved upstream yet?"

"Yes, they've moved, but if I go upstairs I can see them from my bedroom window," the woman whined.

The sheriff visited the swimming site and urged the boys to go still farther upstream. They went. But the complaints continued. The lady called at the sheriff's office and reported, "They've moved upstream, but I can still see them with my binoculars from the attic window."

One of the places where we see a twisted curiosity most shockingly displayed is in the public clamor for courtroom seats when a sensational trial is about to be held. Before the beginning of a French trial that promised lurid revelations concerning the passions of some of the principal participants the judge turned to the ladies who packed the courtroom and said, "It may be that you are not acquainted with the sordid things that will be said here, things that no respectable woman should hear. In view of this I ask that all respectable women leave the courtroom." Not one woman budged from her seat. Then the judge turned to an attendant and ordered: "Now that all the respectable women have left, show the remaining women out!"

Peeping, prying, intrusive, and interfering people are examples of the abuse and perversion of curiosity. An old Latin proverb states a profound truth concerning human nature: "The corruption of the best produces the worst." When curiosity goes astray and becomes deranged, it expresses itself in mean inquisitiveness, in a craving to know the worst.

But when curiosity is nobly used it produces scientific discovery and encourages religious faith. The advances of science have been contingent upon the curiosity of the scientists who

36

have put it to work in careful, patient, persistent investigation. The craving to know inspired navigators to range unknown seas and to discover new worlds. It invited Marconi to work on wireless telegraphy and Alexander Bell to invent the telephone. Curiosity summoned the intelligence and dedication of George Washington Carver to unravel mysteries of goodness buried in the peanut and sweet potato. Dr. Andrew Fleming, curious about mold on the edge of a dish, followed his questions to the discovery of penicillin. Most of the men and women who have benefited mankind through discovery have been prompted by a consecrated curiosity.

But more significantly, a holy curiosity has been at the heart of religious faith. From the beginning of man's sojourn here we have hungrily sought answers to such mysteries as "Whence have I come?" "Who made me?" "To whom do I belong?" "Whither am I headed?" "What is expected of me while I am here?" The life of faith is lived in answer to such questions.

The rapid spread of Christianity in the first century can be largely credited to the power of early Christians to excite the curiosity of the pagan world. Those first Christians made their neighbors ask questions: "How do these Christians come by their love for one another and for their enemies?" "Where do they get their courage to face martyrdom, while praying for their persecutors?" "Why do Christians accompany their dead to the grave with songs of rejoicing rather than with loud lamentations?" "What does Christ mean to them?"

Christianity had the power to arouse the curiosity of the world.

Perhaps the world can be redeemed only when people of faith compel the world to ask such questions.

Does your faith arouse such curiosity?

Do you make people ask such questions?

PART 3:
SEEING OTHERS AS THEY ARE

10

How Can We Handle Human Conflict?

I N THE PAST FEW HOURS A NUMBING COLD wave, accompanied by snow freezing into ice, has been sweeping the country east of the Rocky Mountains. State police warn against unnecessary driving on the highways because of "slippery, hazardous conditions." Radio and television reports have been reaching us, telling of schools closing and meetings being canceled so that people will not need to travel over the treacherous roads.

We are sometimes coached by clergymen and amateur psychologists to "learn to live without friction." Now, with the roads and sidewalks covered with ice, we can get a faint idea of what a frictionless existence would be like, if such were at all possible. At the very least, living without friction would mean living without walking and without any kind of transportation. For walking is possible only as our feet are somewhat abrasive to the ground, and riding is possible only when wheels meet some opposition from the road.

Far from being an evil thing, friction is sometimes desirable and even necessary. So now city sidewalk crews and road workers are toiling overtime, restoring some friction to places where men walk and ride, pouring sand where the friction is most needed on hills and at stopping places.

Of course, while too little friction is disastrous, too much is also harmful, for too much friction produces heat, wears out tires, shoes, machinery, frays clothes, chafes skin, and causes the performance of much useless work. So we lubricate with oils and greases to overcome needless friction. We attempt to reduce it wherever it is destructive.

What about friction in human relationships? Can we learn to live together without friction? No. Should we if we could? Of course not. Most of us have had the uncomfortable and frustrating experience of dealing with some "slippery" character who was such a "smoothie" that we could not grasp exactly what he meant when he talked, what he really intended when he made a promise, or how dependable his word was when he entered into an agreement. He was frictionless, and therefore as dangerous to deal with as an icy sidewalk. We have known, too, of marriages where it was boasted there was "never a word of disagreement." And we felt sorry because of it. How monotonous! Or, how timid! (One large, muscular woman once told me that her husband, a mere wisp of a fellow, had "never spoken a sharp word to me in all our years of marriage." I nearly answered, "He wouldn't dare!")

Our attempts to avoid all friction in human relationships can be ruinous. Parents who dread conflict of wills with their children may become overly permissive, letting children have their own way, thus leaving them unfit for a world where they will not always get their own way. Such children are unprepared to face frustration and are unskilled in the arts of accepting opposition gracefully.

Some people compromise principle and morals in order to avoid friction with those whose favor and high regard they crave. Thus they undermine personality and character.

Vital human relationships, such as exist in marriage, the family, work, professional and business contacts, church and civic functions, political life and sports, mean differences of opinion, aggressiveness, conflict of interests. How can we endure such friction without too much wear and tear on our spirits and without fraying the bonds that unite us?

40

Goodwill is the answer. At the heart of a Christian's relationships with others is goodwill, literally "willing the good" of others and working for that good. Goodwill means desiring the best for others, for those who are in one's own family and those outside it; toward citizens of one's nation and toward aliens; toward one's own race and people of other races; toward friends and enemies.

Goodwill is the Christian alternative to hostility. As Paul put it in writing to the church at Rome, "Bless those who persecute you; bless and do not curse them," as if to say, "You are certain to take some attitude toward those with whom you come in conflict. Choose the Christlike attitude. Bless them."

The year after Benjamin Franklin was appointed Clerk of the General Assembly, a member made a speech against him. Franklin did not punish the speaker by answering him, although, with his wit, Franklin could have withered the man before his peers. Instead, Ben Franklin wrote his opponent, asking to borrow a certain book the man owned. When the gentleman sent the book, Franklin wrote a warm letter of appreciation. After this exchange the men began visiting one another and soon became good friends. This was Benjamin Franklin's way of exercising goodwill. At the moment there was no favor Franklin could do for his antagonist, so he asked a favor of him, thus opening the gates of communication between them. Franklin blessed his enemy with an assurance that an unfriendly act had not hopelessly divided them.

Goodwill is the awareness that all people, like little children, need love most when they deserve it least.

Goodwill means knowing that the secret of many a person's strength is in having a friend, and attempting to *be* that friend. It means going to a person with help when all the world seems to have left him.

Goodwill is the capacity to identify ourselves with others so completely that we treat them as our own. Such goodwill gets its best chance for a vivid expression when we deal with those who are of a different nationality, another race, who speak a different tongue or are of a different religion.

After the Nazis invaded Holland and established ghettos for the Jews in Amsterdam, many of the wealthy, aristocratic genteel Dutch left their homes and went to live in the ghettos with the Jews to share their humiliation. And in Denmark, when the Nazis issued an edict demanding Jews must wear an identifying yellow patch on their sleeves, the king of the Danes, a Christian, put on a yellow armband bearing the star of David.

Such goodwill breaks the tethers that have kept men from appreciating their fellow men, and destroys the foolish encumbrances that have caused unnecessary friction, that have wasted our emotions, chafed our spirits, and wearied our souls. Goodwill such as that shown by the Dutch and the Danish king does not constitute agreement with others, but it permits us to treat those with whom we disagree as our own. They are members of our family, belonging to the same Father, thus deserving our loving care.

It is certain there will always be friction in human relationships. But it will not wear our spirits or destroy us if, by God's grace, we wish and pray and work for the best in the lives of all whom we touch. This is the meaning of goodwill.

11

A Unified Universe

NOW, IN LATE SPRING, ONE CAN UNDERSTAND why God sank back in rest upon the seventh day. Creation never seems more overwhelmingly exhausting than when spring blends into summer and the scrambling, tumbling, multiform shapes, sizes, and species of new life bursting into glad being upon the earth make more apparent the incredible variety, the intricate design, the orderly arrangement of life in the world. No wonder Genesis says that when the Creator had fashioned the world, "God rested"!

Even creating the springtime inhabitants of a forty-acre plot like the one where I now muse would seem to tire the Almighty. Already I have lost count of the kinds of birds I have seen and the varieties of bird songs I have heard since this year's first days of spring. And the species of grasses and flowers, of sedges and ferns, mosses and lichens that timidly peep from the earth as the sun warms their sleeping places are beyond enumeration. Young life teems in the woods, swims in the stream, plays at the entrance of hillside dens. Young things frolic and suckle and sleep and grow. The variety and energy represented here is quite enough to make even the Creator catch His breath and sigh in relief when all this new life seems safely on its way toward fulfillment.

But still more wondrous than the incalculable assortment of living things to be found on one small woodland plot is the way that seemingly independent pieces of the natural world fit together, making sense, unity, and wholeness, like scattered pieces of an intricate jigsaw puzzle brought together by a perceptive mind and a deft hand. To the last small detail all woodland events and all woodland creatures here bear significant relationship to each other, as do all events and all creatures throughout the world. The humidity of the atmosphere, the direction of the wind, the amount of light reaching the forest floor, the chemistry of the soil, all have their reason for being as they are and where they are, and all have their effects. Caterpillars feeding on a particular apple tree leaf and insect larvae under a certain stone in the stream, the chickadee mother tending her young in the hollow of a birch, the doe and twin fawns drinking from the brook, the male fox squandering the afternoon snoozing on a scatter-rug of shade obligingly spread by yonder spruce — all these belong to each other and to the skillfully assembled, unified universe.

The acidity of water in Edgewood Pond depends upon the character of the soil in the surrounding woods, and in turn the welfare of the trout in the pond depends, in part, upon the acidity of the water that environs them. Yet the character of the soil has been affected by leaves, branches, and trees that

CHICKADEES

BOBWHITE QUAIL

RING-NECKED
PHEASANT

RUFFED GROUSE

died and fell and formed forest loam hundreds of years ago. Today's trout are thus meaningfully related to the trees that grew here centuries before Christ was born. In nature ancient times and the present moment belong to each other.

The bright, torchlike scarlet tanager now calling from a distant birch copse brings to these northern acres, and burns here, energies stored from his winter feeding in far-off South America. When the summer passes he and his offspring will take Northern Michigan sunshine back to his winter resort in Bolivia or Peru, so that next December small particles of Hidden Brook, stowed away in a scarlet tanager, will flit from tree to tree in a sunny glade beneath the Equator. In nature our neatly contrived human boundaries vanish as the distant and the near are blended by the essential oneness of the world.

Now, in our time, man, too — once so seemingly independent, going his own way, being as different as he pleased, or dared, or needed to be, living in wigwams here and igloos up there and caves over there, raising rice in Asia, yams in Africa, maize in North America — man, too, is beginning to recognize what was always dimly true of him, that we belong to each other. We are bound together by such vibrating nerves of intercommunication that impulses in Americans are felt by Argentinians and Australians. President Johnson and Mao Tse-tung act and react to each other like next-door neighbors without a fence in between. You and I and Ivanoff cannot let more than a few hours go by without wondering what "the neighbors are doing now," meaning the Russians and the Americans. Humanity shares a common nervous system. Pinch the human race in the Congo and it is felt in Chicago, Cologne, and Calcutta.

In such a world, what you are and where you are affects what a man can be, where he is, halfway around the globe. As the tormented nineteenth-century poet-scientist Francis Thompson claimed,

BLUE JAY

GREAT HORNED OWL

> All things by immortal power,
>   near or far,
> Hiddenly to each other linked
>   are,
> That thou canst not stir a flower
>   without troubling a star.

DUCKS OF ALL KINDS

In a world like this where our complex interrelatedness causes us to hurt and be hurt, to help and be helped, by influences far beyond our sight, does any sensitive soul dare to live less than his best?

CROWS

12

Christian Love Is Hardy

WITH THE ARRIVAL OF SPRINGTIME THE WEAK-
nesses and the hardiness of perennial plants are plainly
shown. Some have endured the hardships of winter admirably,
an achievement that merits the horticulturist's accolade, "hardy." Others have withered and died under the assaults of winter winds, ice, and snow. The hardiness of a plant is its ability
to endure such adversity.

Low temperatures, or quick changes in temperature, are especially hard on plants. Portions of twigs and branches may kill-back because of freezing. Evergreen trees frequently suffer from winter burn caused by low supplies of moisture in the soil, combined with strong winds and the bright winter sun shining through the cold, crisp, clear atmosphere. Alternate freezing and thawing, which take place in early winter and in early springtime, sometimes damage the root systems of young plants. Plants that are weak because of poor soil and nutritional deficiencies, or because of disease or insect damage, are not likely to endure a hard winter or a drought. But the well-established, healthy plant finds ways of conserving its energies and maintaining some flicker of life throughout the ordeal of cold, snow, or dryness.

The hardiness of a plant can hardly be proven under ideal greenhouse conditions. Only adversity tests a plant's vigor and toughness.

As winter tests the hardiness of plants, so sustained, extended adversity is a revealer of virtue and character. A sure sign of spiritual well-being is the ability to endure *prolonged* hardship and to come through the protracted affliction in good spiritual health. A person who achieves this is a hardy soul.

Many a man has had the courage necessary to plunge into a river and rescue a drowning man and has still lacked the durable valor that is required to be daringly uncompromising in the long haul of living every day by high principles. Durable courage is more rare than quick, crisis courage.

Many a woman has passionately fallen in love on a springtime moonlit night but could not stay in love through marriage's tensions, disappointments, frustrations, and desperations. Instant attraction may be more common than abiding affection and lasting love.

The real test of love comes when we attempt to love unlikable people and to *continue* to love them — people who irritate, baffle, thwart, bore, or hate us. Especially is this so if the unlikable person is nearly inescapable, such as an employer upon whom we are dependent for a livelihood, a neighbor from whom we cannot move away, an in-law who lives near us or with us, or a mate whose disposition has changed over the years toward fretfulness or grouchiness. Is our love hardy enough to endure such a spell of inclement weather?

Of course, we can answer that question only after we determine what love is. Human love takes many forms. In the Greek New Testament essentially three words were used for love. "Eros" was the word used to express sensual love, passionate love between the sexes. Another word, "philia," designated spontaneous affection for a friend or relative. (In this sense one might say, "John is such a wonderful fellow. You would love him the first time you met him. Everybody does.") But the great word for love in the New Testament is "agape," which denotes a persistent, patient, merciful, and generous goodwill toward men. Such a love is different from merely liking a person, which may be an involuntary emotion, quite beyond human control. Liking waxes and wanes, flourishes and dies. But "agape" is a benevolence toward one's fellows that aims at actively securing their well-being, regardless of how they respond to us and regardless of their worthiness. It is more a principle of action than a passionate emotion. It is there when they are distasteful and repugnant to us. In short, this highest kind of love is *hardy*.

In the cherished love chapter of the Bible, the thirteenth chapter of First Corinthians, the New Testament affirms, "Love bears all things, believes all things, endures all things." It claims that the life of faith is one where the longsuffering of God is reflected in the patience of His children. As the King James Version of this chapter says, love "suffereth long and is kind." To love, then, in this Christian sense, is not necessarily to like another, to enjoy his company or to share his views, no more than God always finds us delightful companions or in agreement with His viewpoints. God's love is unconditional and operates when we are least deserving and most disagreeable. It is openhearted and generous, and it is bestowed upon those who least deserve it. It is a hardy love.

To love the unlikable means to recognize that we have

48

been loved by God when God has found us unlikable and unlike Him. In gratitude for such grace we pass it on to others.

This discouraging era calls for undiscourageable goodwill, put to action. How is yours? Hardy?

A CERTAIN TOWN IN THE MIDWEST IS BUILDING a new cemetery. Although the village itself has less than three thousand people, its cemetery, the city of the dead, has a population several times that number. So now the city fathers have found it necessary to build a new cemetery to accommodate the graves that will be dug in the coming years. This town is solving a problem that is common in America: as villages and cities age, the more extensive their cemeteries must become.

We also need some cemeteries of another sort — for burying dead deeds, insults and injuries suffered at the hands of our fellow man. When a disturbing deed is done, when its impact and influence have been felt, and when it becomes a thing of yesterday and yesteryear, it should be deeply buried in forgiveness and forgetfulness. If not, it will poison our days.

One of the strangest features of man is the lengths to which he will go to try to keep a past offense alive. He will massage it. He will give it artificial respiration, attempt to pump life into it and breathe fresh irritation, anger and resentment into it, long after the act is finished and its pulse has stopped. Men won't let a dead deed rest in decent peace. Everyone needs a cemetery where slights and injuries can be laid to rest.

Near the close of the last century a traveler named Jones dined at a Harvey restaurant at La Junta, Colorado. Steaks were offered on the menu, but Jones insisted upon substituting

49

-KOHN-

beans. Under Harvey restaurant rules the man got his beans, but was charged the price of a steak dinner.

Jones protested that the beans were worth but a dime. But the manager said seventy-five cents was the charge and Jones must pay it. Jones did. He was in a towering rage when he left the restaurant and stepped aboard the train to resume his journey. After several hours passed, the restaurant received a collect wire and, upon paying eighty-five cents, the manager learned Mr. Jones was still angry.

A few hours later the manager received another collect telegram, paid two dollars and a quarter, and was informed Jones was still resentful. Days passed. Then came a collect wire from Mexico City. The restaurant manager opened it and read, "I still think you charged too much for the beans." It was signed, "Jones."

A man who was eager to make a six-month tour of Europe went to a bank where he had done business for many years and asked to borrow enough money to cover his expenses. The bank refused to make the loan.

Disgusted and angry, the man went to another bank, applied for the loan and got it. He then purchased a five-pound fish, had it well wrapped, returned to the first bank, put it in his safety deposit box and with a twisted, vengeful smirk left town for his six-month European tour.

Such fantastic instances of revenge reveal the absurd extremes to which people will go in attempts to keep hate alive. But other instances are more sad than silly. Take for example the tragic flaw of vengeance in the character of one of the world's best-known poets. Heinrich Heine, the German lyric poet, although capable of producing songs of the most exquisite beauty, sometimes stooped to writing unfair, bitter attacks upon those who disagreed with him. He frequently wasted his genius on cutting satires vented against his enemies.

Heine once wrote, "My nature is the most peaceful in the world. All I ask is a simple cottage, a decent bed, good food, some flowers in front of my window, and a few trees beside my door. Then if God wanted to make me wholly happy, he would let me enjoy the spectacle of six or seven of my enemies dangling from those trees. I would forgive them all the wrongs they have done me — forgive them from the bottom of my heart, for we must forgive our enemies. But not until they are hanged!" Such "forgiveness" is a hollow, mad mockery. It is rankest hatred, mislabeled.

What is wrong with revenge?

Vengeance is primitive, terribly old-fashioned and out of date. Taking personal revenge is the most ancient form of attempting to administer justice. Early in man's history private wrongs were avenged by the person wronged or by his close relative. There was no attempt to render just punishment by impartial judges, and no rules for retaliation. Revenge was often disproportionate to the offense; in vengeance for some petty insult a man might kill another.

Then ancient societies began attempts at limiting retaliation. "An eye for an eye, and a tooth for a tooth" was one of the first curbs placed on vengeance. The Code of Hammurabi, written about 2100 B.C., and the book of Exodus contain this rule for limiting expressions of revenge. Under this rule two eyes could not be taken in revenge for the loss of one, or all of a person's teeth in retaliation for a tooth or two. Later came formulas for compensation of offenses, for the payment of damages: so much money must be paid for causing a person to lose the sight of an eye; another amount was fixed for the loss of a hand. Later still came courts of justice administered by people who were not directly affected by the offense and thus could judge impartially. Gradually we have reached the level where punishment alone is not the aim of justice, but we seek reformation and aim to lead the offender to an honest, wholesome way of living.

Personal revenge is wrong, then, partly because it pushes us back to man's primitive position, before Christ, before Moses; we devolve to where we were at our worst.

Christian faith and practice have always recognized that revenge degrades the person who tolerates its presence in his heart. Christ condemned vengefulness, not only because it could lead to harming the offender, but because it always hurts the heart of the offended. He denounced grudgefulness because the life of faith aims to elevate man and grudgefulness always debauches him. Forgiveness is a friend of reason, while vengefulness is its enemy. Forgiveness lightens life's load, while grudgefulness adds to it, for a grudge is one of life's heaviest burdens. Forgiveness and forgetfulness heal, while the spirit of revenge keeps breaking open old wounds. So the Christian aim is to bury the offensive deed in forgiveness and forgetfulness.

But how can we bury someone's offensive deed in forgetfulness? By "forgive and forget" we do not mean to say that hurtful experiences should be repressed into our subconscious minds where they are out of control and may rankle and ruin us. Rather, Christian forgetfulness means the abandonment of all emotion associated with offensive experiences. It is God's attitude toward His children. As Jeremiah puts it, "I will forgive their iniquity, and I will remember their sin no more." Jeremiah did not mean that God is absent-minded about man's transgressions, but only that He treats the penitent *as if the offense had never occurred.* Such forgetfulness in human relationships does not suggest that hurtful experiences are beyond our recall, but rather that we behave toward our offenders as if the harm had not been done. We remember the offense with the same detachment that marks our remembrance of our house number, our telephone number, the kind of car we drive. The incident, when thought of at all, is seen with a simple, honest clarity, uncomplicated by hatred or desire for revenge. Intellectually we recall the event, but emotionally we forget.

Strangely, paradoxically, this kind of forgetting comes by

remembering! It is the result of filling the mind so full of worthy things that we have no room for emotion-packed recollections of yesterday's offenses.

A most meaningful phrase is found in Paul's letter to the Philippians: "One thing I do, forgetting what lies behind and straining forward to what lies ahead, I press on toward the goal of the prize of the upward call of God in Christ Jesus." No one ever forgets by keeping his attention fixed on the thing he wishes to forget. We forget by becoming attentive to something else. Paul knew that forgetting and remembering are related. He forgot the disturbing elements of his past by filling his mind with the importance of his goal.

We can "forget to remember" the grievances we have suffered at the hands of others by remembering how general and widespread human weakness is. We remember our own faults, recalling that while they may not be identical with those of our offender, they may be fully as irritating and hurtful. We remember how often we have been forgiven by man and by God, and we recall the patience of our parents, our spouses, our children, friends, employers, employees, and all others who have overlooked our blunders and ill temper and have acted as if we had never bothered them.

Have you been treated unjustly? Did someone betray your confidence? Were you slighted or shunned socially or publicly humiliated? Did someone outwit you or "sting" you in a business deal? Do you feel rejected by someone upon whose affection you have depended?

Do you feel vengeful and like getting even? Forget it! Bury the hard feeling under memories of your own faults, your own continuing need for pardon. Cover the grudge with remembrance of the offender's need.

Jesus' command "Love your enemies and pray for them that persecute you" is not only gospel admonition but sound technique. Who can hate a person while earnestly praying for his good? Bury offenses under a heap of prayer.

14

No Matter How Big the Bay

THE GRASSY BLUFFS OF MICHIGAN'S WESTERN
shore seem meant for a musing man. There lovely
stretches, dappled with sun and shadow, are drenched with a
great quietness. One spot in particular is a serene and spacious
place where bright and clear beneath me some hundred yards
away magnificent Lake Michigan stretches wide its blue and
emerald waters from the pale dune beaches of Indiana and
Illinois to the rolling Straits of Mackinac, from the mist-
hunted bays of Michigan to Wisconsin's balsam-shaded shores.

I suspect that the peacefulness of this place has something
to do with the immensities spread in extravagant abundance
here. The bright sky is wide and high. The waters are lavish
and inexhaustible. Nature's generosity with space and sky
and water are impressive here. Nothing is crabbed, stingy,
mean, or small. Everything is liberal, especially the wide
sky and the vast waters, reminding the visitor of the infinity
of time rolling back to the eternity that lies behind today's
dawn and the eternity reaching far out beyond tonight's sunset.

Seeing the great lake always gives me a fresh perspective.
Its very bigness shames human littleness. A look at the lake
adjusts one's feelings of self-importance: waters could swallow
the most conceited fellow and hardly interrupt the murmur
of a wave. This lake view is good for one's anxiety, for by
constrast it makes most big worries seem small matters, and
small worries seem trivial. And an hour on this bluff is good
for one's religion, for it is hard to be thoughtful here and
remain religiously bigoted. In such a place one is reminded

that no one man or no one church or denomination can know all about God any more than any one person from any particular shore can see all of Lake Michigan. The biggest things in life are too great to be entirely grasped or contained by one person, one group, or one institution.

Religion is like the mighty lake that washes and rinses our shores. Lake Michigan possesses awesome, blue-green depths and bright, clear, amber shallows. These great waters sweep into many bays — Grand Traverse Bay, Little Traverse Bay, Big Bay de Noc, Little Bay de Noc, Green Bay, and all the others, and Lake Michigan takes the shape of every depth and shallow, of the big bays and the little coves into which it flows.

One bay is not as good as another. There are wide, deep, hospitable bays that bid cordial welcome to the greatest ships and where the largest vessels can safely ride. Other bays are narrow, pinched, and stingy, or shallow, marshy, and trivial. But the well-informed person knows that it is the same Lake Michigan that fills the greatest depths and the thinnest shallows and all the bays, big and small. How much less interesting Lake Michigan would be if it were simply a mighty saucepan, all the same depth, or if all the bays were just alike, as if cut by the same vast cookie-cutter.

So it is with individuals and with churches. Why should we demand of our acquaintances and friends that they conform to our particular pattern of religious thinking? Or why should Christians insist that all churches worship according to the same ritual and adopt the same formal creeds if they are to be recognized as Christian churches? No one man or woman among us is God; we cannot contain God. No single church or denomination is God, but each is a baylike receptacle, receiving some of God.

This does not mean that "one church is as good as another" any more than all bays of our neighboring lake are of equal value. Rather we mean that we need to develop a capacity for appreciating God wherever He appears, as we already recognize Lake Michigan no matter how big or little the bay.

PART 4:
THE EYES OF FAITH

15

Greater Fruitfulness

T HE APPLE TREES IN OUR SMALL ORCHARD ARE
short, wizened, and arthritic looking, but they are prolifical-
ly fruitful, as the deer have long since discovered. Now in May
they blossom bountifully. Fruit will hang heavy in the trans-
parent, crystal air of September. Boughs will bend low within
reach of browsing deer. Limbs will release well-ripened apples
that tumble into the long grass, there to await the approach of
hungry whitetails.

It has always astonished me to see how many apples one
diminutive tree can bear. Some apple growers contend that
smallness of the tree's structure and fruitfulness are related.
Big apple trees are often too much absorbed in producing
wood to give much botanical attention to yielding fruit. When
the early orchardists in Maine had trouble with their apple
trees growing too fast while producing little fruit, they used
to correct the difficulty by wounding the tree. With a mighty
swing of an axe they cut a deep gash in the tree trunk.
Orchardists claimed that when an apple tree was hurt in this
way the tree changed for the better. Instead of growing into
a big woody plant, it converted its energy into greater fruitfulness and an abundance of apples.

Some people are like erring apple trees that misdirect their

energies into accumulating of quantity. Such folk seem
to think that what counts most is the number of years they
live rather than the quality of their lives. Others measure life
in terms of growth of material possessions, the amassing of
things. Then some deep wound is sustained. A hurtful disappointment or a profound sorrow gashes them and they become
suddenly aware of quality. No more do they care to produce merely more wood. They become fruitful. Far from
being final disasters that destroy them, disappointment and
sorrow become wounds that save them.

Could it be that our hurts are intended to enhance the
quality of our living?

Do our wounds tend toward fruitfulness?

16

Beyond Appearances

ON THESE JUNE EVENINGS THE EMERALD TWI-
light of the forest throbs with woodthrush song as these
brown-winged trumpeters play "taps" at day's ending. "The sun
has set" — so we say. The stars "come out," we observe. But
where has the sun set, and from whence do the stars come? These
expressions hearken back through many a yesteryear to days
when men trusted to appearances and expressed themselves
accordingly. Now we know the sun does not set in the west
or anywhere else but disappears from sight as the earth re-
volves. Far from setting, the sun travels on its tireless journey
while we sleep. Nor do the stars "come out" of anywhere. They
were all day where they are tonight, but the greater light of
the sun dimmed them. Now, with no competition from the
blazing orb, the gentler lights of heaven sparkle like sequins
against the black velvet sky.

The naturalist soon learns to distrust his eyes. He sees
the sun as a yellow-orange disk in the sky, but he knows appearances are deceptive. The sun seems to be a huge yellowish
star only because the longer light waves (red, orange, and
yellow) pass more readily through intervening space than do
the others. The naturalist is aware that while a sunflower seed
looks like a dead and insignificant thing, the truth is that
life slumbers lightly within the seed, life that the touch of sun
and rain will snap to wakefulness, and the imprisoned nitrogen,
calcium, phosphorus and iron, thiamine and carotene, niacin
and riboflavin, and vitamins A, B, and D will become expressed in root, stalk, leaves, flower, and another generation
of seeds. Seeds . . . dead things? Only to the superficial
glance. Beyond appearances, seeds are crammed with vitality.

A narrow driveway only appears to widen when you look
at it with a snow shovel in your hands. A row of garden
radishes only seems to lengthen when you begin to weed it on

your hands and knees. The driveway and the row of vegetables remain the same. It is your attitude toward them that has changed.

We confuse bigness with greatness and size with significance. Because the large things appear to be great and the sizable things seem important we let their appearances fix their value. Christianity changes the world's deceptive standard of values, placing them in reverse order: the unimportant appearing cup of water given to the thirsty becomes strangely meaningful; the weak becomes strong; the meek inherit the earth; he who is greatest is the servant of all.

We never know the whole story. If we appear in court we are asked to "tell the truth, the whole truth, and nothing but the truth." But no one knows "the whole truth" about anything. As Henri Fabre said, "Human knowledge will be erased from the archives of the world before we possess the last word about even a gnat."

Always there lurks beyond the face of things some further truth still unknown. Sir Joseph Stamp, the economist, once told of a candidate for Parliament who approached a house in his district and saw two small children standing hand in hand before the cottage door. Both were boys, of identical size and strikingly similar appearance. The political candidate struck up a conversation with them, asking if they were twins.

"No, sir," they replied.

"But you're brothers, aren't you?" the man inquired.

"Yes, sir," they responded.

"Well, how old are you?"

"We are both five years old."

"Heavens! If you are both five and you are brothers you surely are twins."

"No, sir," one of them replied. "We are triplets. Billy's indoors."

Many of our errors in judgment and much of our bigotry are due to our lack of inclusiveness. We think we have seen everything when we have accounted for all that is plainly evident to us at the moment. Concerning "the truth" there is always a missing fact, important to "the whole truth" waiting to be discovered behind the doors.

Perhaps we have here a partial answer to the mystery of trouble in God's world. Why is it that God allows suffering to come our way? If He is loving, why does He permit it? The

61

answers to this ancient problem are many and fragmentary; the full answer will never come to us while we are here on earth. But here is a glimpse, the merest trace of an intimation why suffering is allowed: trouble strips away from life curtains of concealment so that we more clearly see hidden realities. Sir Ernest Shackleton bore witness to this revealing power of trouble when he returned from one of his Antarctic expeditions. Sir Ernest and two other members of the expedition suffered almost unbearable hardship — pain, cold, starvation, and exhaustion — on the bleak continent of ice before they were finally rescued. Enumerating their salvaged possessions as axes and a log book, Sir Ernest said concerning this long period of torment that these were "all the tangible things; but in memories we were rich. We had pierced the veneer of outside things. We have seen God in His glory."

Is this not one of the chief missions of trouble: to pierce "the veneer of outside things"? Look back upon your own life. See if it is not so that trouble peels back the outer layer of appearances and reveals essences. We may live in a world of show, trying to keep pace with others, hoping to impress our acquaintances with a synthetic success. We may live in a kingdom where "things" are on the throne: money and what money will buy, handsome clothes, bigger cars, more pretentious homes. Then let a loved one sicken, a child of ours. Let death hover near. Suddenly the veneer of importance is stripped from the things we thought counted most. How quickly we would gladly give all our material goods, all our prized fame and vaunted pride, to hear one healthy laugh from that child's lips! What counts now is spirit. Your love for that child may be shown in the bestowal of material favors, but the love is spiritual. The surgeon's instruments can be measured and weighed but not his skill nor his knowledge nor his dedication to his life-saving task. They are of the spirit. And in such a crisis the God to whom we have given so little attention in more confident, self-assured hours, the invisible Spirit, counts then.

Bereavement is a time of revelation. At first we judge by

appearances. When the pulse is stilled we say, "The end has come." But then we begin to look beyond appearances and see that what we have called the end is really the beginning. Nothing is lost that ultimately counts most — personality, spirit, good influences. Something about sorrow snatches the thick veil of externalism from things. As James Russell Lowell sang:

> 'Tis sorrow builds the shining ladder up,
> Whose golden rounds are our calamities,
> Whereon our firm feet planting, nearer God
> The spirit climbs and hath its eyes unsealed.
> True it is that Death's face seems stern and cold,
> When he is sent to summon those we love,
> But all God's angels come to us disguised.
> Sorrow and sickness, poverty and death,
> One after other lift their frowning masks,
> And we behold the seraph's face beneath,
> All radiant with the glory and the calm
> Of having looked upon the front of God.

Faith insists that when we look at the world from God's viewpoint our calamities become "golden rounds" of a "shining ladder"; death becomes a gateway to new life; hopeless matters become hopeful; big things become little and the little, big.

One of life's most fundamental lessons is the one faith teaches: nothing is merely what it appears to be; everything is more than it seems to be. Look beyond appearances.

17

On Knowing the Names of Things

WHEN WE WERE VERY YOUNG, ONE OF THE first things we learned to do with words was to speak the names of things. We were taught that a certain lady in the house who fed and dressed, fondled and bathed and put us to bed at night was "Mama," and we learned to call her by that name. The man who held us on his knee and lifted us above his head and chucked us under the chin and showed us ourselves in the mirror was "Daddy."

There were things in the house that had certain shapes and did certain things that we learned to recognize and call by a name — "bottle," "milk," "spoon," "chair," "kitty," "doggy." And past our house moved still other things that were called "boy," "girl," "bird," "car." Before long we could identify all manner of things by name so that we could tell others what we had seen, heard, smelled, and touched. Learning the names of things is one of the most important adventures of the mind. Names help us to recognize and identify what we observe and to communicate our experience to others.

The great and good Quaker philosopher Rufus Jones once told a true story of children whose learning of names had been severely limited. Some years ago, he said, a man who owned a summer cottage on the coast of Maine determined to start a Sunday School class for children who lived on a nearby offshore island. He sailed to the island in his boat, gathered the children together, and began to instruct them in matters of faith. Hardly knowing where to commence, he decided to start with something familiar to all the youngsters. The Atlantic Ocean surrounded their island. They saw it every day. He would begin with the Atlantic. He asked, "How many of you have ever seen the Atlantic Ocean?"

There wasn't a single response. All the children stared at him blankly.

Thinking they had not understood him, he repeated the question: "How many of you have seen the Atlantic Ocean?" No one spoke a word or raised a hand.

The visitor discovered, to his astonishment, that although the children had spent all their lives with the sound of Atlantic surf beating in their ears and with the vast stretches of the Atlantic spread before their eyes, they did not know the name of the waters that environed them.

The disciples of Jesus were good at calling things by their right names, while some of their contemporaries were not. Christ's followers and His enemies alike watched Him helping others when He might have helped Himself. They saw Him busy with God's program for His life. Enemies and friends alike watched Him paint with gracious words and graceful life earth's clearest picture of God. His conduct was a portrait of God; perfect righteousness was drawn there, unvarying patience, undiscourageable goodwill and supreme love. One of Christ's critics totaled up what he had observed and said, "He hath a devil, and is mad." Thomas summed up what he saw by exclaiming as he looked on Jesus, "My Lord and my God."

Enemies and friends of Jesus saw God working in the world

65

through the Man of Galilee, but only a few could identify God and call Him by name.

How about us?

When you feel like scolding, criticizing, and blaming, gossiping, hurting, or cheating, and instead you are kind and considerate, cheerful and fair, be grateful for the restraint; be glad for the change. It is God working in you.

When you find yourself stretching upward, wanting, aching to be better than you were yesterday and to improve beyond what you are today, when you search to know more about yourself, about others, about the world, about God, and when you profoundly wish to live by the best that you already know, recognize the wish for what it is. It is God working in you.

When you feel an impulse to feed the hungry, give drink to the thirsty, clothe the naked, visit the sick and imprisoned, comfort the disappointed, or strengthen the weak, obey the impulse. Do not lightly call it a "whim" or a "notion." It is God working in you.

When you see men of goodwill gladly giving their best years to teach men to live together in liberty, and in justice, forgiveness, mercy, and brotherhood; when you see statesmen conquer greed, restrain anger, and swallow the harsh and bitter word for the sake of peace, be grateful for man's craving for harmony and concord and his longing for fraternity. It is God at work.

When someone very dear to you is deathly sick and recovers, be thankful for modern medicines, for doctors and nurses who were used by a mighty Power to effect the recovery. It is God at work.

When the blind and deaf Helen Keller was small and had learned how to receive messages from others by placing her fingertips on the lips of the speaker, Bishop Phillips Brooks was asked to try to tell her of God and God's love. The handicapped child put her fingertips on the bishop's lips while he talked to her about the God Jesus revealed to the world. The little girl's body stiffened with excitement and she suddenly cried out, "I knew Him; I knew Him! I didn't know His name, but I knew Him!"

Life's greatest adventure is coming to know God and discovering His name.

18
Building Lots

*Some people
constantly complain
about
their
lot in life;
others
build on it.*

19

See for Yourself

A SHORT TIME AGO I RECEIVED FROM AN ELDER-
ly woman an enthusiastic letter, telling of her excited anticipation of the annual flower show to be held in the great
municipal auditorium of her city. Knowing the lady was not in
robust health and that even limited household chores absorbed
nearly all her strength, I could have advised her: "Save your
strength. Stay at home. Tune in on your radio, and you can
doubtlessly pick up a broadcast of the flower show on your local
radio station. You can then enjoy the show while you are doing
your weekly ironing." A foolish suggestion, wouldn't you
think?

No matter how modern the radio, no matter how many
delicate tuning instruments, there would be colors, symmetries,
and fragrances that would not come to that woman over her
radio. Five minutes at a flower show is worth more than five
hours of descriptive reports. Little value can be derived from
flower shows unless you "see for yourself."

There is no satisfying substitute for personal experience
with the good things in life. That is why in the important
matters we invite people to "See for yourself." The Pilgrim
Fathers, seeking religious freedom, finally reached the shores
of America and wrote back to their relatives and friends in
the Old World about their newly found liberty. But the Pil-
grims did not regard their word as bearing final proof. "Come,
see for yourself," they said.

A housewife describes the delicacy of a new cake or salad to
her neighbor, then hands her a copy of the recipe, and exclaims,
"Here, try it. See for yourself." She knows, as the old proverb
puts it, "The proof of the pudding is in the eating."

By seeing for ourselves we make creative use of doubt.
When it is honestly, valiantly tested and tried, doubt leads
to some of the highest and best personal experiences. Galileo

once called doubt "the father of discovery." It is. Belief in
a flat world was doubted, and the world was proven round.
Doubt about "the spontaneous generation" of diseases led
to the discovery of bacteria and germs. Doubt that it was
necessary for patients to suffer through surgery while pain-
fully conscious led to the development of anesthetics. Doubt
that slavery was a God-sanctioned economic necessity led to
its abolition.

The great pioneers of history have been those who doubted
what they had always heard. But they were not content to
to remain doubters. They went into action. They saw for
themselves. And the whole world has been better for their
courage.

Every individual needs such a venturesome spirit if life, for him, is to be vital, vividly real, and authentic. Everyone must pioneer for himself, setting out from where he is into new areas yet unvisited, seeing for himself what is thus far only a report from some other adventurer. Especially is this true of religious living. One reason why religion is vague and unreal to many people is that they are depending almost wholly on second-hand descriptions for their impressions. They read about prayer and hear much talk about prayer, but they seldom pray in any earnest and sustained fashion. They know much *about* churches, but they do not know a church, thoroughly, from being a part of its fellowship and from participating regularly in worship. They admire loyalty from afar and venerate those who have proven true to their convictions, but they have never become committed to an ideal, such as unstinting service to others, and stuck with it through thick and thin, through good moods and foul, when it was easy and when it seemed impossible.

A person can possess a mind ever so full of beautiful sayings and Scripture texts and be overflowing with lovely sentiments, but until he *acts* in accord with his beliefs his life will be unaffected for good.

The life of faith is a life of first-hand experience of God. Such a faith is as different from reading and hearing about God as a breath of fresh air differs from reading or hearing about the chemical composition of the atmosphere. A text-book analysis of the components of air will do your body little good, but a deep breath of the clean out-of-doors will invigorate your body and sweep the cobwebs from your mind. Chemists report life-giving oxygen is found in the atmosphere. When you breathe, you see for yourself. The saints and seers have reported that man can have fellowship with eternal God. Prayer is seeing for yourself.

The world is in profound need of more people who are dissatisfied with reports of flower shows, and every other good and beautiful thing, and insist on seeing for themselves.

20

Can You Look at Life's Darkness and Still Believe in the Light?

RECENTLY I TOOK AN AIRPLANE TRIP ACROSS A stretch of America's Middle West. It was not an auspicious day for flying, but the flight could not wait for fair weather. Leaden clouds darkened the heavens, and winds whipped the air with sadistic frenzy. Before a drop of rain could fall, the earth was already drenched with forebodings of a storm.

But the plane took off as scheduled. In minutes we were lifted above the heavy storm clouds. What a difference that climb of a few thousand feet made in our outlook! When seen from above, the clouds were not black and threatening, but fleecy-white, touched with golden highlights from the sun.

When were the airplane passengers seeing the clouds truly, realistically — when we viewed them from the ground and perceived their darkness, or when we saw them from high in the heavens and beheld their brightness? Was the dark view or the bright view true and real?

Both views were right. Clouds have a shadowy side and a sunlit side, and what an observer sees depends upon whether he is above or below them.

Pessimism and optimism are the extreme, fragmentary views of human existence. The pessimist looks at life from the ground, from the lowest possible station. He sees only the dark underside of all questions, makes a philosophy of his viewpoint, and behaves as if there were no sun above the clouds and no promise of better days to come. The optimist is nearly always airborne. He maintains a view from above the clouds, seeing life as brimming with beauty, ignoring darkness and storms. A great faith is neither always earthbound amidst gloom nor invariably detached from earth and airily cheerful. Rather, it recognizes that clouds are both dark and

71

light, forbidding and beautiful. Such a faith is big enough, realistic and honest enough, appreciative, daring, and hopeful enough, to see, recognize, and weigh the worst and the best, and to believe that if a good God allows both in His universe He must have a purpose and a place for them. So the man of faith makes room in his thinking for the dark *and* the bright.

The pessimist grumbles, "My gasoline tank is three-quarters empty." The optimist happily, carelessly declares, "My tank is one-quarter full." The man of faith knows that such a tank is both three-quarters empty and one-quarter full. Believing that partial views and dwindling supplies alike are unsafe for earth's travels, he drives to the gasoline station and orders, "Fill 'er up!"

The pessimist complains that the lily belongs to the onion family, and the optimist blissfully responds, "No, the onion belongs to the lily family." The man of faith will likely consult an authority, but the answer will make no difference in his gratitude for lilies and onions. He orders onions for his table and grows lilies in his garden and believes they belong to each other and to a common plan for the world, planned by the Creator. The man of faith is inclusive in his appreciations.

A pessimist gloomily counts all the difficulties in his opportunities. The optimist too often ignores the difficulties in his opportunities. The man of faith, fully aware of the difficulties in his opportunities and of the opportunities in his difficulties, believes that God will help him to use the opportunities and difficulties alike for developing a Christlike character.

Faith is not a belief that everything will turn out to please us; rather it is the confidence that no matter how things turn out, God will somehow use the events of our days for His glory and our good, if we will have it so and submit to His will. We do not know, and do not *need* to know, all that will happen to us. But at this moment, and always, we can know in what spirit we will take everything that happens to us. We can accept the worst that comes our way as being gloomily dark on earth's side and bright with opportunity on Heaven's side, forbidding from our viewpoint and bright with hope from God's viewpoint.

A cellar wall in the city of Cologne bears a heartening gospel. Escaped prisoners of war hid in that cellar during

World War II, and one of them left this inscription written there: "I believe in the sun, even when it is not shining. I believe in love, even when feeling it not. I believe in God, even when He is silent." That faith is more realistic than either pessimism or optimism; it is more honest than pessimism and braver than optimism. It knows darkness, but believes in the sun. It experiences emotional numbness, but believes in love. It suffers the silences when Heaven's answers to man's pleadings are delayed, but still trusts in God.

One measure of your faith is whether you can look at life's darkness and yet believe in the Light.

21

A Few Words to the Brokenhearted

*Not every broken thing is irreparably hurt
    by its wound.
Sometimes broken things yield a hidden
    splendor.*

*This glorious earth, the scientists
    now tell us,
Is but a scrap of the central sun
That was broken off countless eons ago.
In such a way
God creates a world.*

*The light of the blazing sun is broken
    into bits
By falling drops of rain, and, lo,
A rainbow hangs suspended in the sky!
When the bark is broken on a maple tree,
And a spile is driven deep
    into the tree's firm flesh,
Then the maple exudes its sweetness.*

Flowers "burst" into bloom.
The shell must be broken
Before the birdling hatches.

Only God knows
What great good
May soon break
From your brokenheartedness.

22

Singing in a Snowstorm

WHIRLING FLAKES SPUN ABOUT ME AS I WALKED among the bare-limbed birches and the evergreens. The air was full of feathery snowflakes, as if the angels had engaged in an hilarious pillow fight, ripping the cases upon each other's halos and showering the earth's floor with goose down. The flurrying fluff spun through the chilled atmosphere driven hard before a westerly wind that rustled the bare birch branches, whined among the balsams, and sang smartly through the hemlocks. The elements were playing a wintry game, but, like roughneck boys who do not know their own strength, they were playing it wildly, with abandon, and with danger that someone would get hurt.

There was something else in the air, something besides swirling snow and boisterous wind. It was the high-pitched, sweet and clear song of a black-capped chickadee. First from swaying cedar limb, then from pitching hemlock sprig, and then from tossing birch bough the little chorister sang, mingling his voice with other boy soprano chickadees whose cheerful song came from a distance, rising above the sound of storm. "Chickadee-dee-dee-dee," he piped. "Chickadee-dee."

The bright notes came in startling contrast to the gray leaden skies. The light sweet song formed a lively accent against the heaviness of the atmosphere. Confidence was in that voice, and triumph too, as if the little black-topped David knew he could slay Goliath Storm with a few smooth round notes. And it seemed that he did. Soon the storm was gone, but the courageous wee warrior was still jumping joyously about, shooting his small music into the now subdued and quiet air.

There is always something beautiful and deeply moving about singing in a storm, whether the songster is a black-capped chickadee on a balsam bough, or a mother with a household of sick children, spreading gaiety all around, or a sunshine-minded

patient chasing shadows from his hospital ward, or a blind Alec Templeton, whose mirthful fingers coax merriment from the concert piano. Our world would be infinitely poorer if it were not for those intrepid souls whose gallant spirits have rejoiced amidst life's icy blasts.

Are you so fortunate as to own Wedgewood pottery? Then you have some of the world's best! But it was made by a company founded by one of history's most unfortunate people. Josiah Wedgewood, potter to the world, was compelled to leave school when but nine years of age. At thirteen he was stricken with smallpox, which crippled him for the remainder of his life. Adversity blustered around him all his years but could not crush his stubborn spirit. His soul envisioned beauty, sang in the storm, and the world is richer for his having lived.

Few men have sung so sweetly amidst life's turbulence as

did Ludwig von Beethoven. Smitten with deafness when near the peak of a great career, he was for a time prostrated by discouragement and broken by disillusionment. Then, while gusts of misfortune still tore at his spirit, Beethoven began composing again, and there poured from his pen music that has cheered the entire world.

At Christmas we sing "Joy to the world, the Lord is come," one of the most spirited and gladsome of all the Christmas carols. These words sound as if they came from a calm and untroubled life, don't they? But no. Isaac Watts, the author of this hymn that expresses our gladness at Christmas time, was well acquainted with adversity. Sick and puny as a baby, he remained frail and delicate all his days. Often so indisposed that he could not serve his congregations, he wrote them pastoral letters that awed his people with their expressions of high courage. Always an enemy of gloom, he wrote an entire book of hymns, most of which are known as "hymns of praise" — paeans of confidence and cheer. In 1748, Isaac Watts' frail health at last gave out. He left behind scores of songs, seventy of which are still in constant use, eloquent memorials to a man whose indomitable spirit sang through the storm.

And what of the millions unknown to fame, whose high spirits rise above low skies and whose grace is stronger than gales? What about you? Frailties of the flesh and mightiness of heart often go together. Tiny, plucky, black-capped chorister, bravely raising your song at the heart of the storm, you remind me of that!

PART 5:
TAKE A CLOSER LOOK AT LIFE

23
Almost!

IN RECENT WEEKS MUCH OF NORTH AMERICA
has suffered from uncommonly severe winter weather.
These subfreezing nights and days, when snow spirals almost
unendingly through the cold blue silences, are critical times for
our wild neighbors. Winter is the season of narrow margins of
safety. These are the days when only five or ten degrees of
temperature, a few extra feathers, a small surplus of fur, an
additional bit of food, and a little spare fat around the ribs
mean much to the creatures of field and forest. Those that
perish will die because they had almost, but not quite enough
warmth, food, and stamina to take them through the winter.
The deer that will starve are those that are only slightly smaller
than other members of the herd and cannot quite reach the
browse that hangs tantalizingly close, only an inch or two
above their outstretched muzzles. Those that survive will
greet the coming spring because they possess a little advantage
in height and strength and have small margins of reserves. We
are passing through the season of "the almosts," when the
dying almost live and the living almost die.

The origin of much of the adventure and drama of life can
be found in its narrow margins, its brinks, verges, and breath-
taking "almosts." Before authorities put a stop to the practice

WINTER BEGINS

The deer are still fat from heavy fall feeding...

WINTER CONTINUES

As the season advances whitetails gather in herds and form "deer yards"...

WINTER ENDS

And in areas whe food scarcity is critic countless deer are o of starvation.

a few years ago, at least thirty-one people attempted death-defying stunts at Niagara Falls, some seeking to pass through the mighty rapids in small boats, others venturing over the deep gorge. Many of these perished. These sensationalists were not seeking death but aiming to come as close as possible to it, knowing that there is incomparable excitement for the participant and the spectators in a hairbreadth escape.

But there are other narrow escapes that are tragic rather than thrilling and plentiful rather than rare. They are the hairbreadth margins by which the best, rather than the worst, is missed. For example, here is a promising young man with a little family. He has recently moved from a small community to a big city to practice his profession. Where he was raised and married he was well known and highly respected, but where he now lives he is almost lost in a world of crowds. Neglecting to establish himself in a fellowship of people whose high standards would lend support to his own, he soon finds himself tempted to desert the old, familiar moral values. He *almost* remains true to the high ideals of his youth. He nearly clings to an early decision that selfless service is better than mere money-making. He comes close to saving his self-respect. And he almost remains faithful to the woman he married — almost.

A boy nearly passes his university examinations, but not quite. An adolescent girl is invited to participate in some devilishness that is beyond all rules of decency. But goodness, honor, and self-respect are attractive to her, too. She nearly says "no" to evil enticements and "yes" to the call of the Highest — almost, but not quite.

A carload of young people speed down a highway at one o'clock one Saturday morning. The driver loses control of the car on slippery pavement, then almost regains control, but not quite. Four of the youngsters lose their lives when the car hurtles into a tree.

Somehow it wouldn't seem quite so bad if these people had encountered a disaster that was wholly, utterly unavoidable. But how disappointing and sad to be almost acceptable at college, almost admirable and good, almost spared from accident, and then to miss being saved by so slight a margin.

If we fail at being what we ought to be and at doing what we ought to do, isn't our failure usually by a small margin? The spectacular failures are few. The slight failures are plentiful. You know some of them — the people who almost win promotions, nearly become leaders, narrowly miss being winsome or even saintly.

The difference between the great achievers and the mediocre performers is small, but that little "edge" distinguishes between the champion and all others. The world-champion hundred-yard-dash sprinter can run that distance only a few seconds faster than many a local boy can run it. The world's best jumper can leap only a few inches higher than some high school athletes you know. Men have won the presidency of the United States by receiving only a few thousand more votes than their opponents. But how consequential the little differences can be!

In a world where narrow margins make wide differences, how should we live? We must aim at the *maximum* kind of life. The miserable are those who live by minimal standards, just inside the law, those who merely manage to hold their marriages together without ever making real homes of their houses, and those whose spiritual exercises are not enough to make them strong but consist of an occasional, polite, neighborly nod in God's direction.

Those who live abundantly do for their world far more than the law requires, giving more than the minimum. In their community they are not content to bear the name "citizen" when they have merely paid taxes. They work for the general welfare far beyond the call of duty. In marriage they do not insist, "I will go halfway and that's all. Marriage is a fifty-fifty proposition." Instead they behave as if marriage were a hundred-hundred proposition, where each partner is solely responsible for its success. And the welfare of their souls is nourished by more than a mere trickle of meditation and prayer. Their spiritual roots grow deep into inexhaustible supplies of wonder, reverence, gratitude, trust, joy, and peace, resulting in *more than enough* vitality and power for all their common days and for any emergency life can offer.

The welfare of the spirit, like that of the body, rests upon having more health than is absolutely necessary. This is what we mean by resistance — reserves of health beyond the demands of ordinary, everyday life. We are constantly pelted with germs from our environment, but probably more than 99 percent of the germs that fall upon healthy human beings die within the first ten minutes. What kills them? Health does. A healthy body simply does not meet the conditions upon which

82

most germs thrive. The best way to kill germs is to strengthen the organism upon which they attempt to grow. So it is with temptations toward meanness, smallness in dealing with others or moral looseness. We invite trouble when we are minimal Christians, lukewarm or spiritually anemic. Evil thrives on the person who is almost healthy, but not quite. But evil has little chance of success in the soul of one who is wholehearted, utterly dedicated to God and spiritually healthy.

In the light of this necessity for maximal spiritual health, one can almost hear God speaking to us in the words of a romantic song of yesteryear, "Take good care of yourself: you belong to me!"

24

Clearing Up Foggy Notions

A PERSON CAN BE LOST AND STILL HAVE A *general* idea of where he is. His problem is he does not know his position in any *precise* way.

I well recall a late January day twelve years ago when my friend Oscar and I tramped across the frosty forty acres where our home now stands. I had seen the place briefly a few days before, and had fallen madly in love with its groves of birches and stands of cedar, spruce, and balsam, and with its irrepressibly joyful brook skipping among the rolling hills. Now I was hoping to purchase the land and build a cottage there, but I wanted Oscar, a former farmer and experienced woodsman, to evaluate the acreage for me.

Snow was lightly falling when we walked through the gate. But by the time we had trudged four hundred yards, we were in the thick of a blizzard so blinding that we could barely sight each other, although we were walking side by side.

We were certain there was a fence bounding the property, and we knew of the creek flowing diagonally across the land, cutting through the birch groves. But exactly where we were in relation to the main road, the gate and the car, we had no idea. Our tracks had been wiped out by the driving wind and drifts of snow, so that we could not retrace our steps. Where was the trail? Where was the gate? Where was the road?

In general we were in Section 27 of Hayes Township, Charlevoix County, State of Michigan. But no such vague generalities helped us much.

Soon we figured how we could get to the main road where the car awaited us. If we managed to walk in a straight line, we would surely come to the creek or a fence. And if we reached the creek first, we would follow it until it led us to the fence, and by tracing the fence far enough we would reach the gate. Sure enough, the plan worked. A particular stream

guided us to a certain fence that led to a definite spot where stood a gate and an automobile we were most happy to see.

Amelia Earhart's last words, radioed in 1937 from her plane over the Pacific, were these: "Position doubtful." Miss Earhart's problem was that she had only a vague idea of where she was. In general, she knew she was flying over the Pacific, but she had no precise knowledge of her location. Indefiniteness as to where we are is perilous.

Someone may argue that uncertainty is useful on rare occasions. Perhaps! Diplomatic language is often purposefully vague and obscure. A diplomat declares, "My government will strongly oppose any and all attempts. . . ." But he does not make clear what he means by "oppose." Will his government issue a verbal protest? A written objection? Will the matter be taken to the Security Council of the United Nations? Will diplomatic relations be severed, and will ambassadors be withdrawn? Will an economic boycott be imposed, or will shots be fired? What does "oppose" mean? The diplomat prefers not to say. Vagueness has value for him. Keep the world guessing.

In the late 1800's, P. T. Barnum's New York museum was a popular attraction and occasionally became overcrowded by customers who were prone to linger too long. Barnum solved the problem by building a corridor to the doorway that led to the street. At the entrance to the corridor he prominently displayed a sign, TO THE EGRESS. Since nearly no one knew the meaning of "egress," the curious crowd surged toward the sign and out into the street before they discovered that an egress is an exit.

Such uses of vagueness as are made by diplomats and showmen may be either helpful or humorous. But most vagueness leaves us lost in uncertainty, "in the woods" or "at sea," which is always unpleasant and often tragic.

One of our greatest needs is to rid our minds of unnecessary vagueness. Our inner nature demands some clear certainties. The worst kind of anxiety is what some psychiatrists call a "floating anxiety," a vague sense of fear and dread about nearly everything in general but toward no one thing in particular. Many a patient with floating anxiety has improved upon breaking a leg or upon having an operation for appendicitis or gallstones. The reason? The break or surgery has rid the person of a vague, fretful, and worrisome anxiety. The floating anxiety has come to rest upon a specific physical problem.

Countless people have wasted many years of their lives wandering from one job to another, stumbling from one religion to another, blundering from one marriage to another because they were vague as to what they really wanted out of life. More than a few have been redeemed by discovering some central certainty.

Clarity is necessary to spiritual progress. No one can win a football or basketball game unless he knows where the goalposts or baskets are. Spiritual progress comes from knowing where we are in relation to the standards and ideals toward which we are to move. Now, then, how can we replace vagueness with clear certainties?

First, we can insist upon seeing the good life in terms of particulars rather than in terms of unclear generalities. This was what Jesus did and taught. His clarity sometimes troubled His listeners, because a vague, general "righteousness" was less demanding than a call to specific deeds of love and mercy, of justice and self-giving.

The word "neighbor" had a warm, comfortable sound as long as it was not clear who was included by the term. When Jesus was asked by a lawyer, "Who is my neighbor?" He answered by telling a parable of a foreigner who became for all time "the Good Samaritan." You remember the story, how a "certain man," whose name and nationality, race and religion are not given, was set upon by robbers, badly beaten, his goods stolen from him, and he was left near death. A priest passed by, but did not help the victim. A Levite, one of special sanctity and purity, saw the wounded man, but offered him no assistance. Then came the Samaritan who demonstrated what it means to be a neighbor. This half-breed, a member of a society discountenanced by Jesus' own people, was not a neighbor in general, but a neighbor in particular. He anointed and dressed the stranger's wounds, placed him on his beast of burden, took him to an inn, paid his expenses, and watched over him. The neighbor was anyone and everyone in need and anyone and everyone who would serve that need. But Jesus made the point clear by describing "a certain man" and his particular predicament, and by telling of his Samaritan helper and precisely what he did to render assistance. The Samaritan preferred specific deeds of mercy to vague feelings of soft sentiment toward the unfortunate.

On another occasion when Jesus spoke of compassionate goodness He talked in specific terms. He clarified the meaning of kindness by mentioning particulars: a gift of food, a cooling drink, a welcome to a stranger, clothing for the poor, a visit to the sick and the imprisoned (see Matthew 25). These are concrete examples, demonstrating that loving kindness is not a generalized sentiment to warm the heart, but intense care that seeks expression in particular acts. Instead of inquiring of us, "How do you feel toward others?" Jesus would ask, "Precisely what have you done for others?"

This leads me to say another thing: live the best way you presently know, and then reflect upon your life. Take yesterday's and today's events and deeds; review them one by one. Attempt to interpret them and try to understand what each one means. Some vagueness as to what you really believe will disappear if you are honest about your actions. Your deeds are motion pictures of your beliefs. What do they say about your trust in God and about the position of God above or among all your other loves? What do they say about your beliefs concerning life's purpose and destiny and about service to your fellow men?

Jonathan Daniels once told of a book salesman who tried to sell a farmer in southeast Arkansas a set of books on scientific agriculture. The old gentleman slowly thumbed through the books, then said, "No! I don't want them."

"But you should buy them, sir. If you owned these books you could farm twice as well as you do now."

"Son," the farmer replied, "I don't farm half as good as I know how now!"

Isn't much of our fuzzy thinking about religion and the meaning of our existence due to a reluctance to practice the

best we already know? Do we learn most about mechanics by thinking about mechanics or by doing mechanical work? Do we gain confidence in swimming by reading about swimming, or by plunging into the water and practicing the best we have witnessed and heard about swimming? Every expert swimmer first took a few clumsy strokes. Confidence, certainly, and mastery of the sport came from more and more actual swimming. So with praying, giving, and the performance of compassionate deeds. We learn by doing. .

Vague ideas about great matters become distinct and creeds become clarified when notions are translated into actions.

To get a clear idea of the meaning of your faith, try translating creeds into deeds.

25

Before the Curtain Rises

TOO OFTEN WE ARE LIKE LATECOMERS ENTERing the theater during the second act of a stage play: we miss the beginning and rob ourselves of the full flavor of the drama.

This is true in our observance of nature. We are inclined to notice springtime only when it is well along, when tassels of silvery pussy willows suddenly appear by ditches filled with melting snow; when the first April robins brace themselves on our lawn against the resisting struggle of earthworms, and when marsh hawks return from the South; when the white trillium unfurls and nods in moist May breezes, and spring peepers chorus in the swamp; when smelt "run" in rivers and streamlets and baby raccoons awkwardly scramble down from their lofty cradles in hollow trees. Then spring is plainly here.

But the first act of spring starts many weeks earlier. It opens while snow lies inches thick upon the North, before antlers are shed by the last procrastinating buck deer, while dark limbs of the hardwoods are still naked. Tender twigs of ground shrubs then bear buds, prophetic of next summer's green leaves. Then the deep silences of evergreen forests are stirred by the weird wooing calls of courting barred owls, who are among the first of the bird kingdom to sense the approach of the nesting season. Under the wood's coverlet of snow the first delicate, pale blossoms of hepatica cautiously begin to open. Now, in the second week of April, the plot of spring is well developed. But the observer who first notices spring's arrival now is late in coming to the drama. We are already in the second act.

One of the chief handicaps of being a city dweller is that one seldom sees anything at its beginning. Almost everything comes to a city person in a late stage of development. He rarely sees raw materials. His is a world of finished products. City people eat bread, potatoes, and beef like the rest of us. But how many urbanites arrive at the play of natural forces before the first act begins, when the plow is set deep into the good earth and the long straight furrows are formed and the wheat that is to become bread is sown? Or how many know what it means to plant potatoes and nurse along the vines and protect them from insect pests until the hidden tubers are ripe for digging? How many have studied the breeding of good beef cattle, planned the matings of cow with bull for improvement of the stock, or attended the birth of a Hereford calf that one day will feed a hungry Detroit family and be converted into their flesh and blood? Creation is more than the country man's natural environment: creation is his business. He must be present at the beginning of things.

There is something elemental and indescribably satisfying about being aware of beginnings. I'm sorry for the people who never arrive on the scene in time for the first act: the folk

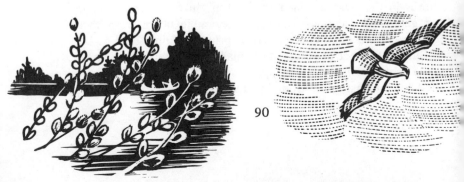

90

who get their dogs half-grown and never knew them during clumsy puppyhood; the people who arise when the morning is half gone and rarely see a dawning and the first twenty minutes of a day; the many who can never appreciate budding possibilities in children that throng our streets but who can only recognize greatness when it has obviously arrived at ripe maturity. The latecomers miss more than half the fun.

An eye for beginnings is a mark of wisdom and goodness. The wise man reflects on what he is tempted to say before it is said. The foolish man reflects on what he has already spoken. The wise man sees the harsh deed budding in his rising temper and checks it. The foolish spends much of his life cleaning up the messes he has made with his passions.

One of the best ways to avoid moral downfall is to recognize the weed of evil while it is a little sprout and to root it up. How many moral collapses could be avoided if the victims would have seen what was coming before the tragedy was in its last stages! The adolescents who engage in "heavy petting" but do not intend to "go all the way"; the politicians who think they must promise almost anything to get votes, although they intend to avoid political corruption; the employee who thinks he can compromise his moral standards in the slightest degree in order to make an advancement in his firm, although he does not intend to become downright hypocritical — all need to remember that he who does not take the first step in the wrong direction cannot take the last one. As Shakespeare cautioned, "Look to the budding mischief before it has time to ripen into maturity."

Life is a Broadway, with many dramas, good and bad, opening and closing all around us. Elemental to our Christian faith is the belief that, if we will have it so, the present moment is

91

the beginning of a new play. Do we want to be better than we are? With our past so sullied with sin, what's the use? Well, under God, the old tragedy can end and a new drama can be enacted. The curtain can rise on a new beginning.

Bishop Bruce Baxter once told of a teacher's asking a class of children, "How many of you can name the four main points on the compass?"

A little lad responded, "Excuse me, teacher, but the compass has *five* chief points."

The teacher replied, "Now I always thought there were only four, but if there are five, you name them."

The youngster said, "North and South, East and West, and the place where you are right now." And the last is as important a point as you will find on the compass. It is the place of beginning again. Dissatisfaction, regret, and penitence may be "where you are right now" but they are the commencement of change. No noble living starts with radiant character and gracious deeds. They come in the second act. At the beginning is the desire to be better. And most of us have that. And we know the One who makes the best Director and who should "call the changes."

Then . . . on with the play!

92

26

Abundant Life

NOW IN MID-SPRING, THE TREES OF NORTH America awaken to the call of returning birds and to the choruses of spring peepers singing in the marshes. Sap rises, bringing renewed life to each tree, like blood commencing circulation in a numb leg that has "gone to sleep."

The tender light of April has coaxed green leaves from the dark buds lining barren limbs. Hills have removed their heavy, white winter coats and have put on light scarves of green. City parks and countrysides are freshened with an emerald mist that has settled on the treetops.

All across the land orchards clothe their naked branches with a superabundance of leaves. Horticulturists estimate that it takes thirty leaves to make a Jonathan apple and fifty to produce a big Delicious apple. About thirty leaves are required to make a large peach. However, mature apple trees will be equipped with about 100,000 leaves apiece, many more than each tree will need to produce its fruit or to do its work of lifting out of the earth four gallons of water per tree each hour.

This abundance of reserve leaves is to make the tree adequate to any time of crisis. Succulent leaves will attract many insects. The larvae of moths, butterflies, sawflies and beetles will attack and consume foliage, reducing the tree's capacity for manufacturing food. So each healthy tree produces a total leaf surface that is far greater than its anticipated need. Thus,

if a considerable portion of its leaves are destroyed, the tree can still survive.

All through nature a tendency can be found to produce reserves. Quail, pheasants, ducks, and other ground-nesting birds lay more eggs than are necessary to perpetuate their race, so that if some eggs are destroyed by marauding crows or plundering skunks or mink, enough will survive to produce a small family. A female brook trout may lay 5,000 eggs to assure the preservation of the species, since some eggs will be infertile and many young will be prey to other fish and will not live to see their first birthday. Nature insists upon reserves to assure continuation of the race.

When man is wise, he too plans upon an abundance of reserves. Merely enough strength to "get by" will never do. When the cables were built to support the weight of the San Francisco-Oakland bridge, they were fashioned with a capability of bearing a load two and one-half times as great as the maximum they would ever be called upon to bear. That is the way to handle all of life. All bridge builders should provide more strength in their structures than they will ever need. All scholars should know more about their subject than any examination will demand. Every long-distance runner needs a "second wind," a reservoir of energy to draw upon when other men's power wanes. A healthy person is one who has more physical reserves than any active day can drain and more than life's crises can exhaust.

What we all greatly need is not a diminishing of problems, but an increase in adequacy. Speaking of His disciples, Jesus said, "I am come that they might have life, and that they might have it more abundantly." Abundant life is no mere "hand to mouth" existence with barely enough caring, forgiveness, patience, and love to get by. Abundance of spiritual life means more than enough power for common daily needs, plus inexhaustible reserves for any crisis that may confront us.

The person who has the abundance of life Christ came to bring us can spend virtue lavishly because his resources are plentiful. He can care for people unreservedly, the people near him and all over the earth, people of his own creed, color, and nationality and those of other faiths, races, and nations, because his resources of care are attached to the limitless reservoirs of God's care.

He can afford to be slighted, shunned, hurt, because he has enough forgiveness in his heart for any crisis that comes his way.

He can be patient when other men's patience is exhausted because he not only has his own patience to draw upon, but God's patience too.

He can squander love upon the undeserving and unresponsive because he knows there will always be more love where the last love came from.

An English poet and essayist, while pleasantly talkative among close friends, was restrained among strangers and casual acquaintances. When a woman complained that he did not readily engage in conversation, he replied, "I have only ninepence in ready money in my pocket, but I can draw a check for a thousand pounds!" He refused to put all his wisdom in a showcase. He had much in reserve.

The Christian faith is one of abundant resources. The man of faith does not need to count on little bits of cash in his spiritual pockets. He can write a check for any amount needed on the account of "God and Company." *That* account is inexhaustible.

95

SQUIRRELS FREQUENTLY MISS LIMBS WHILE JUMPING

GROUSE SOMETIMES SLAM INTO TREES

DEER LOCK ANTLERS WHILE FIGHTING, GET ENTANGLED IN FENCES ... AND WEDGED IN THE CROTCHES OF TREES.

DUCKS, GEESE AND SWANS HIT WIRES AND ARE MAIMED OR DI

27

Failure Is a Badge of Man's Greatness

MAN IS NATURE'S CHIEF BLUNDERER. HE IS THE creature most heavily endowed with a capacity for mistake-making. Man can fail more easily and in a greater variety of ways than can any other animal that walks the earth. Though squirrels have been known to misjudge a distance while leaping from tree to tree and have fallen to the ground, and deer have been known to fatally mistake a stock-still hunter for a harmless stump, no nonhuman, wild creature blunders morally, spiritually, maritally, professionally. Man does. This fact represents both man's tragedy and his glory.

We humans can make mistakes in our relationships that are far-reaching in their consequences beyond anything known in the animal kingdom. When two dogs or cats are mismated, the harm done is relatively limited. But when two people who are wrong for each other marry and have children a long chain of tragedies may be started, the tensions, pressures, quarrels, and divided loyalties affecting the children, and the children's warped personalities affecting their children in turn, and on and on through untold generations and countless tangled human relationships.

The messy morals of a stage or film idol have disastrous effects upon innumerable teenagers who live far from the idol's home.

Hitler's, Mussolini's, and Stalin's moral and political blunders precipitated the agony and death of millions who never saw their faces.

This is man's tragedy, that he can slip, flounder, and fall so wretchedly and with such far-flung consequences.

But it is man's magnificence as well as his misery that he is the world's mistake-maker. His power to make mistakes is indication of his wide range of choices and possibilities. A boy can be manly or bestial. A girl can be ladylike or a brat. But a kitten can be nothing more or less than a cat: its possibilities are strictly limited.

Ministers of religion do not invite creatures other than humans to love God or to follow Christ, because only humans can make a wondrous choice and only humans can refuse God and deny Christ. This is man's glory, that his Creator has made him a creature of wide possibilities for good or evil. Man's capacity to choose the wrong, to make mistakes, to blunder or fail, is a badge of his greatness.

Moreover, man's capacity to blunder witnesses to his God-given courage. Guaranteed success demands no courage. Risky undertakings do. A mistake is proof someone has had the daring to attempt to accomplish something. He makes no mistakes who tries nothing difficult and makes no discoveries. Our greatest failure is to do nothing for fear we will fail. We hesitate to visit the defeated and the grieved for fear we "might say the wrong thing." So we say nothing. We are reluctant to stand up and speak our convictions in public, because we "can't find the right words." Thus we leave great issues weak and floundering for want of our support. The world suffers far less from brave blunders than from man's inertia that comes from his dread of making mistakes.

The best exercise for strengthening courage is that of taking daily risks of making mistakes while attempting to do the will of God through serving the needs of mankind.

Finally, *apparent* failure does not mean *final* failure. James Whistler failed at West Point and, humiliated, left that famous institution. Had he been a success there he might have become a fair army officer. Having failed, he turned to art and became one of the world's most famous painters. His seeming failure did not mean ultimate failure.

On October 12, 1492, Christopher Columbus discovered America. But Columbus had blundered badly. When he reached the east coast of the Bahamas he thought he had sailed to the East Indies and called the natives "Indians." But Columbus was ten thousand miles and two continents away from India and the Indies. He died in the year 1506 still supposing he had reached the East by sailing westward. What a glorious blunder! By his courageous faithfulness to a conviction, he had opened America to the future and had stumbled into an incomparable place in history. His apparent failure was his ultimate success.

Then too, do you remember that the shadow of a cross once spread across the world, spelling the end of Jesus of Nazareth? It *seemed* like the end. To all appearances the cross finished Him and His hopes. He had failed. But we now call each year A.D. — anno Domini, the year of our Lord — as if each year and all our years are now His. The centuries reveal what was hidden on the day of His execution, that apparent failure may mean final victory when God is in control of things.

Our failures, our defeats, and even our un-Christlike blunders can be used to make a better life and a better world, when placed in God's capable hands.

28

Something to Grow On

DO YOU REMEMBER YOUR CHILDHOOD BIRTH-day celebrations, especially the spankings you received from your parents, brothers and sisters, or neighbor children? When you were nine, for example, you were given nine smart whacks on the proper location. But the person administering the paddling did not stop with nine resounding blows. An extra stroke was given with the announcement, "One to be good on," and still another, "One to grow on."

There is a whimsical bit of wisdom in that ending of the traditional birthday spanking. We all need something "to grow on."

Growth toward maturity is a characteristic of all living things, from seeds planted in the fields to fish eggs laid and hatched in lakes, streams, and oceans; from nestling birds hatched in a fern-graced bower of the forest to children playing in nurseries and city parks. Growth is a least common denominator of all living creatures born into the world; growth is the development of the hidden potentialities, the secret qualities that we bring into the world when we arrive here.

But everything that grows must have something "to grow on." If a farmer wishes to grow corn he must determine what the corn will grow on, what fields offer the best type of soil, where the soil will be most uniform, well drained, nutritious, and best suited to bring out the full potential of the seed. It is not enough to want to grow corn. Corn must have something to grow on.

So it is with growth of mind and spirit. The letter to the Ephesians advises early Christians, "We are to grow up in every way unto him who is the head, even Christ." But what are we to *grow on?*

We grow on fellowship. We wither and die through detachment from other people, and we thrive on the good we

find in those to whom we belong. One of our primary joys is found in accepting and being accepted, approving and being approved, appreciating and being appreciated, forgiving and being forgiven, in the company of those we respect and love.

The best things in life come through sharing. Art is shared

beauty. Education is shared truth. The church and its services of worship, hospitals and their missions of mercy, charitable institutions and their help for the needy represent shared goodness. There would be no painting, sculpture, music, no schools, churches, hospitals, no charity, without a craving for and a fulfillment of fellowship. By eating, playing, working, and worshipping together we partake of the powers we find in members of our family, our neighborhood, and the larger circles of society. Through great books, great art, great music, we keep company with the best minds of all time, and these souls that touch ours leave some grace, some good, some inspiration and aspiration as nutriment for our spirits.

When we are engaged in splendid fellowships, the company we keep keeps us. We grow on the fellowships we form.

We grow on our necessities. Necessity is an ugly word, signifying the restraints we shun, the unavoidables we wish to avoid, and the inevitables we seek to evade. But necessity is deceptive. It hides the nature of life's inevitables. Necessity is like some weirdly disguised character at a masquerade party. Its guise is frighteningly like that of some demon from the nether regions. But when masks are removed we see necessity is no devil at all but one of our best friends.

Hardly any baby bird learns to fly simply because it has a yearning to do so. Fledgling birds remain in their nests and beg their parents to feed them as long as the adults will yield to the hunger cries of their young. But soon comes the moment when the parent bird senses that the nestlings are mature enough to fly and she pushes them from the nest. The fledglings first learn to fly from the starkest necessity, and only after that can they fly because they desire to fly. They fly because they must before they fly because they wish.

God must sometimes confront us with necessities before we can become what we should be. We pray for patience, but God never sends us ready-made patience in gift-wrapped packages. Rather He allows us to get into situations where patience is the answer. A newspaper delivery boy accidentally throws the *Daily News* through a porch window; the wife is slow with dinner; an employee confuses the office bookkeeping; our four-year-old son scribbles on the nursery wall with red and yellow crayons; the husband is irritatingly forgetful; Grandpa grumbles about every little thing. Patience has no chance to grow when life is smooth and pleasant. Frustrations are what patience grows on. They make patience a necessity if we are to live decently and gracefully.

It is dangerous to pray for better character unless we really mean business, for God will permit some necessity to come our way that will give character something to grow on. If we ask for courage, He will give us something on which to grow courage — some temptation toward conformity to man's will, some fear that needs to be overthrown. If we plead for strength some burdens will come our way. Strength will grow by lifting the burdens. Necessities are what we grow on.

God will ripen and mature the possibilities for good He has fashioned in all of us. So He sets us in a world of fellowships and of necessities, hopeful that we will draw from them the nourishment that will stimulate and sustain our growth toward Christlikeness.

29

When Roots Are Intertwined

SEVERAL YEARS AGO AN ACQUAINTANCE OF mine purchased a beautiful piece of property on the shadow-dappled rim of one of Michigan's largest inland lakes. His location was heavily wooded, so in order to clear a building site he hired a bulldozer operator to push over most of the trees with his heavy equipment. When the trees had been uprooted, they were sawed up and the trimmings were burned. All that were left were a few choice spruces, balsams, and white birches. Then in the clearing a house was built, with a breath-taking view of the lake. But before many months had passed, a ground-soaking rain, lasting several days, saturated

and softened the resorter's lawn. Then followed a day of fierce howling winds, and most of the choice trees the resorter had saved for beauty's sake toppled to the ground. He had not realized that the roots of the choicest trees had been intertwined with the roots of the trees he had ordered removed. When the dispensable trees were bulldozed off the property, the root systems of the beautiful evergreens and graceful birches still standing were disturbed, wrenched, and weakened. Rains and winds completed the havoc the bulldozer had started.

Now birches grow singly and in clusters along the brook that rambles past my study window. So do maples and poplars, balsams, spruce, and hemlocks. The stream's bank is soaked with moisture from the brook, and the soil has been softened by tiny drops that creep amidst and infiltrate particles of earth. One would think that the streamside would be unsafe for trees in time of wind. But that is not so. These brookside trees have known a thousand storms. They have wrestled with every bullying wind that challenged their courage and disputed their strength. But I have never known one to tumble to a storm. Age and disease take their toll, of course, as they do of all living things. But in a sudden crisis these brook-loving trees are not storm-dazzled or vanquished, and for this reason: their roots are intertwined. They support each other. The crooked fingers of birch roots reach out for other roots and find in them an added strength. The hidden, knobby hands of evergreens and hardwoods secretly, urgently stretch for the reinforcing, reassuring grip of neighboring trees. There seems to be a kind of deep awareness in Hidden Brook trees that if they are to be strong enough to survive wind-shock and tempest they must depend upon a strength greater than their own. So they reach out to their fellows. Hidden Brook trees do not rely upon solitary strength. Their quiet, confident mien in windy weather rests upon a fellowship of roots. Each tree's strength is reinforced, being intertwined with the strength of others.

One way human beings build power for surviving crises is through joining the roots of being with the roots of others around them. In this way the strength of others supports us and our strength supports others. A trend has developed in modern psychiatry to maneuver patients into wholesome associations with good personalities. Psychiatrists and psychoanalysts have come to see that the treatment of a patient as a solitary problem-person is inadequate. If he is to gain strength, it must come from somewhere, and a good source is the goodness of his fellows.

Public worship is such an experience, the roots of the spirit urgently reaching out and embracing the staunch roots of others. Worship is a fellowship of faith. Through hymns and anthems and Scripture reading our faith meets the faith of others of times past. We exercise a "communion of saints" in which our hope is reinforced by another's hope. Our trust in God is no longer a lone, solitary thing, but part of an intermingled network where our reasons for trusting are augmented by the witness of many another believer. Testimony supports testimony. Faith sustains faith. We see that we are not alone in our struggle to be better; there are others with us.

Books provide means for intertwining the roots of our lives with the roots of the great people of history. Literature brings to us the thoughts of Moses, the faith of Jeremiah, the understanding and spirit of Christ, the distilled experience of Paul, the reflections of Shakespeare and Milton. Biography refreshes us with insights into the undaunted courage of Washington, the undiscourageable magnanimity of Lincoln, the awesome dignity of Robert E. Lee. James Russell Lowell once asked, "Have you ever considered what the ability to read means? It is the key that admits us to the company of saint and sage, of the wisest and the wittiest at their wisest and wittiest moment." Good reading admits the best in us to fellowship with the best in the great people of all time. Through literature the power of great lives reaches across space and time and strengthens us; their roots mingle with our own.

One of the secrets of successful living is to make the habit of reaching out for fellowship with the highest, most wholesome people we know — the triumphant, the wise, the humble,

107

the self-forgetful, the creators of the beautiful and the appreciators of beauty, knowing that they have something of value for us, as did One who promised, "My peace I give unto you."

But besides seeking out such people, we must aim to be the kind of person who strengthens. Just as successful marriage is not alone the business of finding the right partner but one of being the right sort of mate, so the world's good is not served alone by our making connections with the best people; we must be the kind of persons from whom others can derive power.

30

Hunt the Hot Spots

OUTDOORSMEN KNOW THAT IF THEY WISH TO find wild game they must not look at random for the creatures of forest and field, because wild animals and birds do not live at random. They thrive only where life's essentials, such as food, warmth, and shelter, can be found in abundance.

Naturalists are also aware that many of our wild animal neighbors favor the so-called "hot spots" situated in almost any wilderness area. Hot spots are small localities, often not more than a few yards square, where the temperature is usually a few degrees above that of the surrounding territory. The place may be sheltered from winds by dense evergreen boughs. It may be a sunlit hillside exposure. Usually vegetation for food and concealment grows luxuriously in such salutary surroundings. To such places animals and birds withdraw to dine and rest.

When visitors to my woodland study ask if there are deer on our acreage I sometimes take them to one of these hot spots and often our search is rewarded. More frequently, however, I see deer in the woods near my Hidden Brook study when I'm not looking for deer at all. Instead, I may be tracing the call of a strange bird, or walking to the nearby pond to feed tame trout, or I may be just enjoying a breath of the out-of-doors. At such moments I catch a glimpse of a deer drinking from the pond or bounding off through a sun-warmed forest glade. Sometimes if I simply stand still a deer will walk within a few feet of me without noticing my presence. Nearly all of my favorite natural haunts are hot spots, frequented by all kinds of birds and beasts, especially white-tailed deer.

The search for happiness is a little like looking for wild game in the woods. There is no sense at all in seeking for either wildlife or happiness in places that are inhospitable to it. But there are hot spots where one can expect game or gladness to be found. Moreover, happiness is like the furred and feathered children of the wild: it is elusive when chased for its own sake; but while we are seeking something else worthwhile, happiness makes its appearance. Sometimes it walks right up to us. We may suddenly find happiness looking over our shoulder when we are overcoming a handicap or learning to tolerate one; when we are mastering a hardship or transmuting pain into power; when we are risking our reputation to save that of someone else from senseless, vicious assault; when we are cheering a child who has broken his best-loved toy or lost his dog; when we are carrying a light into someone's grief-darkened day; when we are fighting for an ideal or kneeling at an altar. Look for things more important than happiness, and happiness will make its appearance, fairly begging to be recognized.

In Psalm 144 the writer joyfully exclaims, "Happy the people whose God is the Lord!" God wants His children to be happy. He has strewn the earth with places where happiness thrives. Sometimes, however, the children of God are miserable because they seek happiness in places inhospitable to it. They are like foolish hunters looking for gray squirrels on the Sahara, for tigers in the Arctic or for polar bears in the jungles of Africa.

Where are life's hot spots, where happiness is found, where happiness finds us?

DEER LOVE MAPLE BROWSINGS

CEDAR IS HIGH ON THEIR WINTER MENU

ACORNS ARE AMONG THEIR FAVORITE FOODS

DEER LIKE FORESTS   **...... AND OPENINGS**

... HIGH LAND   **... AND LOW**

Look upward for happiness. The Psalmist was right: "Happy is the people whose God is the Lord!" Gladness comes from the recognition that there is a Power available to us beyond our small store of strength. There is a Care for us that is more abundant than our self-concern, and a Forgiveness greater than our sin. Look up!

Look inside. Happiness thrives on the good that is inside a person rather than on the good fortune he hopes to find around him. Happiness is found in fulfillment of one's real inner capacities: the ability to appreciate and create the beautiful, to know the truth, to develop toward a greater goodness, to make one's place on earth better than it was on one's arrival. Unhappiness comes from blaming ourselves because we are not more capable, criticizing our environment because it is lacking in appreciation of the little we do. We do not hear opportunity knocking because we are knocking much louder. Look inside. See what is there that the world can use. Use it for the world's sake and for God's sake.

Look around you, into the present moment and the immediate situation. Happiness is found in the here and now. Those people are most miserable who moan for yesterdays that are past or who put off living until some bright tomorrow when life will be exactly right for enjoyment. We defer delighting in life until conditions are improved. We think happiness is off yonder somewhere, and we will find it when we get married or get unmarried; when we find a better job or have more money; when we feel better physically; when we are better known; when we are anywhere else but here and it is any time but now. Thus we miss the happiness that is lurking in the present conditions, waiting to be recognized. The most miserable people on earth are those who have everything they once wanted, and still lack one thing, the ability to appreciate it. The happiest people are the appreciators. They find enjoyment where they are. They lose their painful self-consciousness while finding in everyday circumstances worthwhile things to do, worthwhile causes to serve, worthwhile people to love, and they see God everywhere.

112

PART 6:
THE UPWARD LOOK

31

A Man Is as Big as
the Things That Move Him

IN SPRING WE SEE ELEMENTAL EVENTS TAK-
ing effect among us. Spring is a time of hatchings and
births, with life getting a fresh start in myriad ponds and
streams, in nests and dens. It is a time of revolution, when
April and May conquer the tyranny of winter, life breaks the
rule of death, springtime overthrows the kingdom of gloom,
and man feels sunlight reaching into the very marrow of his
bones.

Now, in May, we behold a blending of man's response to
earth and earth's response to man. It is this fundamental
transaction of business between man and earth that makes
spring the most exciting season of the year. In the yellow-
green hours of springtime man acts and expects nature to
react appropriately. The boy raises his kite to the strong,
moist breezes; the householder cleans out last year's nesting
box and hangs it again in a tree near the house; a special stall
is prepared for a mare to have her colt and for a cow to
bear her calf. The lawn is raked; the garden is spaded; the
field is ploughed; the gardener plants his bulbs and the farmer
sows his seeds. And each performs his task with high expectation as if to say, "If I call, Nature will answer."

Agriculture is based upon the assumption that there is

D. Edmond Hiebert
Collection

something beyond us that is sympathetic to us and sensitive to
what we do. The farmer ploughs and plants and then waits for
Nature's reply to his expectations. He believes that the silver
rains and golden sun will encourage the good earth to ac-
knowledge his work and answer his trust with growth and an
abundant provision for his need. All great religious faith
rests upon the idea that behind this responsiveness of Nature
there is a God who cares for us and answers our need, and
that Nature is but one of His ways of manifesting His concern.

Responsiveness is a basic element in human nature. Man's
very physical being is fashioned for sensitivity to what the
world may be saying to him. We have lungs for responding
to air, ears for responding to sound, eyes for responding to

light. Air, sound, and light were here before man came, and lungs, ears, and eyes are God's way of furnishing man with an answer to the atmosphere and a reply to the visible, audible wonders of the world.

One of the world's saddest sights is a person who can make no appropriate response. We have all seen such a person at one time or another. We may have watched with pity as a mother awaited the first sign that her infant recognized her and would smile at her in answer to her smile, and we have seen grief steal into her face from her fearful heart as she realized the child might be blind, or mentally retarded, and could not respond to her as she had hoped.

Then there are others who will not respond when they can,

the pupils in school who will not listen to instruction, the citizens who will not bother to vote even when they know great issues are at stake, the tourists who speed through vistas of breath-taking beauty oblivious to the splendor because they are preoccupied with the number of miles they can travel each day. Unresponsive folk are as frustrating as were the dolls about which one little girl complained to her mother, "I just love them and love them, and they never love me back."

Jesus had trouble with such doll-like, dehumanized, unresponsive people. In the days of His flesh He "went about doing good," the book of Acts tells us. But He could not do the good He desired *everywhere*. Why? Because some people were unimpressed by Him. They did not receive Him with eagerness and high expectation. The Gospel of Matthew cites Christ's rejection by His neighbors in Nazareth, His own home town: "He did not do many mighty works there, because of their unbelief." Some knew Him too well, so they thought. They were His neighbors and relatives. He had a familiar face and manner. He had worked for them in the carpenter's shop, making their doors, tables, and chairs. How could God do anything of real consequence through such a commonplace fellow? The power of Christ was present among them in abundance, but the Nazarenes missed it because they lacked the faith to respond to it. It takes little faith to respond with amazement and joy to miracles that occur across seas, or a province away, but to behold God's work — and to appreciate it — when it is a next-door miracle, seen every day, *that* occurs only to rare souls.

Man is made to respond, and we are hardly human at all until we are humble and awe-struck in the presence of God and God's wondrous works. God reaches out to us through the beauty that surrounds us, through the prayers of those who love us, through the example of some walking gospel whose life we have read, through the Bible, through a well-trained conscience, in manifold other ways, and supremely through Jesus Christ. At our best, we eagerly reply. We answer in wonder, in prayer, in changed and devoted ethical conduct. "We love . . . because he first loved us," declares the First Epistle of John. God's love takes the initiative and man answers. And this is man's glory, that he can sense God's care and His commands and is capable of grateful, joyful response.

A man's soul can be measured by the size of the things that move him. The greatest souls are those who appropriately respond to God.

32
Rest Your Soul in a Patch of Light

SOME OF OUR FOUR-LEGGED FRIENDS HAVE a habit that we humans could well develop for our spiritual profit. They make a practice of playing and resting in a patch of light. Not far from my study desk is a sunlit knoll where long ago a vixen fox dug her den on the south side of a hill where the sun peeks through an opening in the encircling trees. There in the spring of each year fox cubs frolic upon the sun-drenched grasses and wrestle among the sun-warmed ferns.

On a dark day, when the sun bursts through a rift in heavy storm clouds, our dog Lass will find a small circle of sunshine where a few rays drift through our windows. There she will lie, basking in a soft, warm splendor.

When we are at our best we humans do a similar thing. We seek out a sunny spot of spiritual light and warmth, and from time to time we return there and allow our minds to play in the golden radiance or let our souls rest in the beneficent warmth.

This is one way we encourage the growth of faith. We let memory spread light from the past upon our present situation. In that patch of light the mind plays and rests. When days were dark with discouragement, the ancient Jews would recall the admonition of the book of Deuteronomy, "Remember the day when thou camest forth out of Egypt," and "Remember the way which the Lord thy God led thee." The Israelites had been slaves of the Egyptians, but God freed them. If God could help them in such an extremity in the past, He could help them again in their present or future distresses. What God had done He could still do. In that thought their souls stretched and grew, rejoiced and found repose.

An old gospel song advises, "Count your blessings, name them one by one." Reviewing the good that has befallen us lets the best hours of our yesterdays — past joys, companionships, and victories — warm the present moment. Some cheering word of a friend, a gay note of remembered laughter, or some thoughtful act of kindness restores our faith in what other people can mean to us. An illness overcome, a temptation resisted, a sin forgiven, a tragedy turned into triumph refreshes our trust in God's ever-present help. "Remember all the way which the Lord thy God led thee." In such ways our souls play and rest in a patch of light from the past.

But more is involved here than the use of the past to brighten the present. Choosing a patch of light in which to play and rest also means selecting from the *present* those things most worthy of our reflection and our faith. This world is filled with strange mixtures of good and evil, of light and dark. We shall be in touch with both the best and the worst. Being "realistic" does not mean, as we are sometimes led to believe, to look at life's dark or vulgar side, interpreting the worst as "reality." The true realist looks at life as it is, as the biblical faith sees it, with its slavery in Egypt and its day of emancipation, with its sin and redemption, its squalor and splendor. And the person of faith then chooses to stretch his soul in the sunny awareness of the mercy that is here amidst life's mischief, and the Redeemer who is present amidst the ruins.

Well, then, let's face reality. Our mental health and our spiritual good depend upon it. But reality must include the best as well as the worst aspects of our human situation. A cesspool is real, but so is the clean, happy brook that sings and dances past our cabin door. Promiscuousness and adul-

tery can be found in almost any community if one looks hard enough, but so can pure living and marital faithfulness. Grudgefulness and revenge are here in the world, but so are forgiveness and grace. Cruel gossip can be heard almost anywhere; so can sincere words of appreciation and honest praise. Profanity is real; so is prayer. War is hideously real, but peacemaking is real, too. Judas is no more real than Jesus. Crucifixion is real; so is resurrection.

When sunlight streams through our windows, Lass seeks out a patch of radiance and basks in its warm splendor.

Where does your spirit find rest?

33

Of Course Miracles Happen!

MAY DECLARES, "MIRACLES DO HAPPEN!"
A May day is beyond man's explanation. Almost anyone can account, in a rough way, for the arrival of spring
by citing known "laws" of nature and by showing how more
warmth is brought to our hemisphere as this area of the world
turns toward the sun. But such an interpretation of spring's
coming in no way diminishes our wonder as we watch May
merrily frolic toward June. A whiff of a dew-laden meadow
or a fragrance of apple blossoms drifting on morning breezes,
the sight of a shy nodding trillium hiding on the forest floor,
transcends every written law and defies all description and
explanation. Uncommonly beautiful things appear in this
extraordinary month, things that are signs that point upward,
reminding us that the Creator is still creating, prompting us
to remember how dependent is earth on Heaven.

Man has not brought May to the earth. May days come before man named the month and before man was here. Man
can neither halt nor hurry May's coming. Maybe this is one
reason this month seems so wondrously good: it wholesomely
reminds man of his limitations and of the Power that works
beyond man's limitations. In a world where we are unduly
impressed by our inventiveness, technology and gadgetry, in
May we are peculiarly aware that all the turbines, dynamos,
and industrial plants in the world cannot develop one-quarter
horsepower of capacity for causing a yellow lady slipper to
blossom or for compelling a forest fern to unfold. Man can
do little to hasten, slow, or stop the throbbing pulse of nature
as it beats out the seasons. In a thousand other ways we influence nature, tearing up turf and causing erosion, massacring
forests and creating floods, moving mountains with bulldozers
and dulling the scenery, until we feel well-nigh almighty. But
no man, or combination of men, ever made a May day.

The biblical meaning of miracle is not the meaning most common today, which implies an event that is a contravention of nature. In the biblical view a miracle was any wonder that was a sign of God's working among His children. A miracle was a revelation, not just any wonder but a *luminous* wonder that shed light into man's dark ignorance of God and God's ways. Like a May day a miracle pointed upward and reminded man of things above him. Miracles of healing of body and mind demonstrated that man was not alone with his ailments and afflictions. God cared and God could manifest His care, sometimes by performing surprising wonders of healing or, again, by supplying wondrous capacity for endurance and cheerfulness under the burden of infirmity. Either way, men knew that only God's help could offer any plausible explanation of the mystery of restored health or a reinforced spirit.

The Gospel of John tells of a Pharisee named Nicodemus who came to Jesus one night and exclaimed, "We know that thou art a teacher come from God; for no man can do these miracles that thou doest, except God be with him." The Revised Standard Version of the verse uses the word "signs" where the King James Version says "miracles." The word "signs" clarifies "miracles," for in the Bible a miracle is more than an event that seems to break through the natural order or passes understanding and is bewilderingly wondrous. Rather, like a wayside sign, a miracle calls attention to something beside itself, as a sign saying "Riverside, 63 miles" is not meant to advertise itself, but the distance to Riverside, California. A sign saying "Mount Rushmore Memorial" is not intended primarily to draw attention to the marker, but to the mountaintop and its vast sculpture of America's president-heroes. Christ's miracles were not mainly meant to make men mindful of astonishing healings and exorcisms, but rather to signal the good news that God cares for His children, and He watches over them with loving care all along. The extraordinary, miraculous event is the *unusual* sign that points to the *usual,* the astonishing reminder of the love that is always there but which we so easily forget.

122

The miracle of Christ's life is a sign signifying God is in our midst, among us, the Word made flesh. God always loved us enough to dwell among us and always will. Christ's miraculous life was God's remarkable, singular way of pointing this out to us clearly and once and for all.

Nicodemus cited another aspect of miracles when he said, "No man can do these miracles that thou doest except God be with him." A miracle, then, in the biblical sense declares this truth: that which is beyond human power to accomplish unaided can still be achieved through the help of God. "Except God be with him" is a key phrase; a miracle points to the assistance of God.

It reminds us that man's unaided efforts are inadequate to handle the world, to do what must be done, to answer his own deepest needs for healing of body, mind, and spirit, for comfort, forgiveness, renewal. We need reinforcement by a Power beyond our limitations. No one ever heals himself by will power. Everyone relies upon forces beyond effort alone. Even the physician does. He gives medicine or performs surgery; then he waits. Nature (man's weak word for God) must do the rest.

No farmer grows crops by sheer physical effort. Hammering a seed or squeezing it in a vise will not make it grow. Every farmer must sow and then step back and count upon God and His beneficent forces of sunlight, rain, and fertile soil. When looked upon religiously, every growing thing, like every healed body, is a miracle — a sign of the wonders God constantly performs beyond man's strength to achieve.

The works of the masters of the fine arts are witnesses to this truth about miracles. We say that the artist Raphael, the sculptor Rodin, the composer Johann Sebastian Bach, the dramatist Shakespeare were "gifted." Gifted how? There can be no gifts without a Giver. The great masterpieces are miracles in the biblical sense, for they represent a Power that is beyond what human exertion can create. If effort alone could produce enduring works of art, every art school, school of music, and writing class would be pouring out a deluge of masterpieces, for the schools are full of pupils who try hard enough. But the world's best artists are not known for their effort alone. They are primarily known for their gifts. "No one can do these miracles . . . except God be with him."

The miraculous life is one that sees the signs that God is ever present, and lets such a God-consciousness control every aspect of one's existence.

The Universe Goes on Its Mighty Way

MAN HAS RUN AND STUMBLED PELL-MELL TO-ward "progress," scratching the earth with hoe and bull-dozer, defiling the atmosphere with smoking campfires, belching chimneys and bursting super-bombs, but still the universe moves on, undiscouraged, as May days joyfully testify.

Yesterday afternoon, for the briefest spell of a moment, two bits of bright orange flame illumined our streamside birches. The tiny bonfires were borne on the breasts of Baltimore orioles that yearly visit these acres, search for a home site, and build their pendant nests from the limberest of limbs where woods winds can lullaby their young. Orioles likely darted among Hidden Brook trees before the first atom bomb fell upon Japan, before the cry went up from American throats, "Remember the Maine," before the Revolutionary battles of Lexington and Concord, before the white man landed on these shores, before Christ was born or Moses descended Mount Sinai with sacred tablets of stone.

This morning our shower-swollen stream charges past my study window, unmindful of me. If I should cast a fly upon its waters, hoping to lure a wily trout, the stream would dimple in fleeting acknowledgment, then erase the mark and hurry on its tumbling way toward the nearby lake, singing of timeless things as if this creature of time did not exist.

May reminds us that the universe goes on its mighty way without significant interruptions. Earth's prodigious labor of pushing up plants is never frustrated by strikes, when the soil sulks, or when butterflies, birds, and bees tire of slaving for the flowers and demand higher pay and shorter working hours. Management is liberal, bestowing side benefits in generous profusion: ideal working conditions, bounteous bonuses of nectar and morning dew, musical accompaniment of woodthrush song and silvery tinkle of shower-filled stream, the fragrances of cool, forest-flavored air and the easy-on-the-eyes lighting of blue May skies sifted through the silver-green of leafing trees.

Labor-management relationships are excellent between earth and Owner. I pray they'll improve between man and Maker, so that this little earth, as well as the immense universe, can go on its way.

126

35

A Morning Prayer

Father,
Whose love is wide,
Whose mercy deep,
Thou hast given Thy children sleep,
And now upon the earth outpoured
I see Thy warm light,
Gracious Lord.

127

Through every hour
This day may bring
Let my heart with gladness sing;
Through every moment guard within
And keep my soul
Unstained by sin.

Quietly, as the moments flow,
Let my spirit stretch and grow
Until there's room enough in me
For self,
And all mankind,
And Thee.

36

When New Life Comes

O Holy Father,
Make us ever mindful
　　　　that
As surely as
Each new day
Begins at midnight,
So
The coming of new life
　　　　in us
Follows
　　some
　　deep
　　darkness
　　of
　　the
　　soul.
—Amen—

37

Prayer on an Autumn Day

Eternal Spirit,
Like muted leaves
Upon the amber air
of fall
The russet hours
of autumn
now
drift
past.

Like the coming of leaves
in emerald May,
And their glorious going
in colorful October,
May my days
Gain luster as they linger,
And my hours
brighten
as
they
pass.

As countless plants
Now strew their varied seeds
upon the winds
That, in far-flung places
Where the flowers
themselves
can
never
be,
Their offspring
may beautify
and
grace the earth,
So spread what little good
that I can do
Far from my sight.
Let it spring up
and
yield abundant fruit
In places
never
known
to
me.
—Amen—

38

When the Waters Are Disturbed

FROM MY STUDY WINDOW I LOOK OUT UPON
the unceasing flow of my favorite stream, Wood's Creek,
colored with sun and shadow, winding its way from nearby
springs to a neighboring lake. Upstream a few yards from
our house the brook gently glides through deep, green, spruce-
shaded silences. Directly in front of the window that illumines
my desk the solemn stream suddenly breaks into silvery
laughter as it plays mischievously with logs, stones, and
broken branches and then joyfully skips into a tree-rimmed
opening where today it is greeted with fair skies. A few feet
downstream the water abruptly becomes serious again, dropping
its playthings, forming a tranquil, dreamy pool, perfectly re-
flecting the unmarred images of birches that grace the snow-
cushioned banks. So the stream moves on toward its
rendezvous with yonder lake, slipping through wind-rippled
glades, dancing past snow-and-sun-brightened meadows, frol-
icking lightheartedly in the light, sulking in the shadows.

If one wishes to probe the secrets of a stream like ours,
searching for the multitude of living things that inhabit shadow-
haunted depths and mystery-patterned bottoms — for darters
and daphnia, crayfish and crustacea, brook trout and bryozoa
— the best results are to be found where the waters are most
disturbed. Life is most plentiful and most vital not in the
reposeful silences of still, dark pools or in the peaceful, dreamy
shadows where the stream moves slowly under protective,
overhanging banks, or in quiet, sunlit stretches of the mirror-
surfaced brook where idle clouds leisurely swim on bright
winter afternoons, but in the *troubled turbulences*.

The reason this is so? Where water is most highly agitated
it becomes well supplied with oxygen — a basic necessity for
the sustenance of life. While forests, farms, and swamps
contribute generous supplies of decomposing vegetation to

the streams, adding accumulations of poisoning carbon dioxide and reducing the proportions of oxygen in the water, turbulences caused by water dashing against rocks and dropping over falls replenish supplies of oxygen and make streams habitable. Scientific experts who deal with water and its properties say that swift water swirling among stones, dashing over logs, and cascading down waterfalls is filled with healthful

oxygen because the turbulence creates a vital contrast between water and atmosphere. While stagnant water may be cursed with a deficiency or an excess of certain atmospheric gases, rapid, agitated, disturbed water churns into itself the atmosphere that floats just above it.

Life's turbulence, rightly used, does a similar thing for us: it mixes Heaven into our human situation in a way that peaceful ways never do. Obstacles to our comfort, hindrances to our hopes, distresses, afflictions, misfortunes, griefs — like boulders in a brook — create the kind of disturbance that can churn the Above into the Below, the Spirit of God into the spirit of man. As Benjamin Franklin said, "After crosses and losses men grow humbler and wiser." And Saint Paul, long before Franklin, wrote to the Christians at Corinth about the great good that came from his vexations: "I take pleasure in infirmities, in reproaches, in necessities, in persecutions, in distresses for Christ's sake: for when I am weak, then am I strong."

James Barrie told of his mother suffering cruelly from the death of her eldest son: "She came back to her desolate home and bowed herself before God. But she never recovered from the blow. . . . That is how my mother got her soft face. . . and her pathetic ways, and her large charities, and how other mothers ran to her when they lost a child." So trouble, gloriously used, benefits the soul.

It is not by accident that man's profound thoughts have come through disaster rather than through prosperity; that the noblest expressions of the ancient Hebrews were uttered during the Babylonian capitivity rather than when they were triumphantly expanding the borders of their kingdom; that the most sublime words spoken in America were voiced during the agonizing violence of the Civil War and not during one of America's great economic flourishes. Prolonged success, comfort and pleasure usually stagnate us and fill us with self-poisoning self-centeredness, self-sufficiency and self-content. Troublesome tumult reveals our need. It breaks up our earthly sophistication so that Heaven's answer can be joined to earth's central questions, and Heaven's rich grace can be stirred into our deep spiritual destitution.

Just above our need hovers God's great readiness to help us, like the atmosphere lingering over a flowing stream. It sometimes takes the dashing of our souls against some dreaded obstructions to let the divine resources mingle with our human weakness so that our sluggish souls can be refreshed.

39

Communion with the Skies

A FOREST COMMUNITY HAS AN ASTOUNDING appetite. It is ravenously hungry for energy and must have a constant supply of it. A single acre of beech and maple forest, together with its plants and animals, will each year consume energy equivalent to the electricity needed to supply your home with power for the next half-century. Nearly all the energy entering the forest community comes in the form of sunlight, only one percent of which is manufactured into the chemical energy of food by green plants. (The other ninety-nine percent is dissipated as heat, reflected from the leaves, or spent in some other way.) The food manufactured by the plants, trees, shrubs, grasses, and multiform other living green things is passed through the tissues of plants to plant-eating animals, and from these animals to predators, and from the predators at last to scavengers and then returned to the earth in the form of dead animals and vegetable matter. Some energy in the form of food builds tissue; some becomes fuel to drive the organic engines in animal bodies — the equipment that makes for movement, growth, and reproduction. All day long energy pours into the forest, where some of it is stored in food or in the body tissues of creatures living there, and where some is lost, such as by the giving off of heat by animal bodies.

Life continues in the forest, as elsewhere in our world, because of the daily influx of new energy in the form of sunlight. This is true even on a wintry day when the normal processes of life seem almost suspended, when the sun is far away and disinterested in the welfare of a Northland forest, when even a bewildered little snowflake drifting uncertainly to earth seems more energetic than all the cold light falling on shadowy timber. Yet, on the bitterest winter days the sun is still losing over four million tons of matter per second — matter that is

converted into heat and light. Although the great blazing bon-
fire of the skies is more than ninety million miles away, and
although just now in December its light and heat strike only
a glancing blow on the North, nevertheless its light reaches
out through the cold blue silences to bless all the acres of this
land with nearly two thousand calories of heat per square

foot per minute on the sunniest days and a surprisingly generous measure of heat and light in the gloomiest hours.

Now, in the polar hours, buds continue to develop on knobby limbs. Roots grope deeper into the dark, rich soil, feeding on nutriments found there. Deer browse soundlessly among the long, dark shadows. Winter birds pick up sunshine sandwiches in the form of seeds and insect eggs. The forest and its creatures, on the best days and the worst, gather in their harvest of light and warmth from the distant sun. They can remain alive on earth only if they hold communion with the sky.

An openness to Heaven is the secret of any life worth living. Spiritually exhausted people are those who have no inflow of energy to match their outgo. While trying to make a living they forget how to live. Their busyness is greater than their receptiveness, and they spend too much time in frenzied activity in proportion to their quiet hours of inspiration, prayer, and glad, openhearted hospitality to the Highest. Their lives are not open to the skies and to the sunlight.

In man, as well as forest, life continues by virtue of a vast inflow of power from Above. Keep your spirit open, Heavenward.

40

Star Bath

THE SKY IS PECULIARLY LOVELY ON A FROSTY night when winter lies thick on our roof and window sills. A night wind has shepherded flocks of woolly clouds to some distant celestial fold so that the blue-black heavens above us are clear. Sparkling in cold brilliance in a high and wide silence above the earth the distant stars look down upon frost-bound, snow-drifted land. A slender sliver of new moon drifts dreamily across the sky.

Such a night is meant for wading in thoughts until the wonderer is beyond his depths. It is good for us to lie back awhile, lazily leaning our weight upon deep mysteries, like stumbling in a deep drift of snow, lying there, relishing it and not caring to rise too soon.

Especially after a day of dealing with small details it is good to take such a star bath. We are so prone to become like what we are attentive to that hours spent on minutiae make us small. Punching a time clock, putting parts together on an assembly line, typing reports, tapping keys on an adding machine, correcting computations, fulfilling assignments, preparing and serving meals — all the little features of daily living have a way of dragging our minds down to their size. To achieve and maintain the full stature of manhood and womanhood we need frequently to focus our minds on bigness.

In Florence Barclay's *The Rosary* a doctor says to his patients, "See a few big things. Go in for big things. You will like to remember when you are bothering about pouring water in and out of teacups that Niagara is still flowing." And when we are tired of accounting for where our money went, or wearied of adding up duties still to be performed before the weekend arrives, or bored with planning how many and what guests we should invite to our next party — then it is restful to step outside and attempt to count the stars in the vastness of the sky. Bigness is the best antidote for littleness.

On a clear night, with the unaided eye, from 5,000 to 7,000 stars can be seen throughout the world, only half of them, however, being visible in our half of the sky. But with the help of the 100-inch Mount Wilson telescope approximately 1,500 million can be seen. Look through the two-hundred-inch mirror on the Palomar Mountain telescope and additional billions of stars come into view. Distances to the stars are measured in terms of light years rather than miles. A light year is the distance light will travel in a year's time while speeding at the rate of 186,000 miles per second. In other words, a light year represents a distance of approximately six trillion miles.

The Milky Way, of which our sun and its planets are but a tiny part, is composed of some one hundred billion stars. From our earth to the center of the Milky Way the distance is about fifty thousand light years. If you could go from Charlevoix to the far outer edge of the Milky Way on some heavenly steed, galloping along at the rate of 180,000 miles per second, it would take you 100,000 years to make the trip.

Still, beyond the Milky Way there are other galaxies, yet more vast.

Such a star bath for our thoughts cleanses the mind of the transitory, the little, the insignificant.

Plunging one's thoughts into the immensities of our universe does something else for us, too. It can deepen our religious faith and enlarge our reverence for God. Dr. Henry Norris Russell, famed Princeton University astronomer, once gave a lecture in which he talked of the Milky Way and its millions of stars. He told how many of them are far larger than our sun and how the still more distant heavens swarm with stars innumerable. When he finished his address a troubled woman came to him and asked, "Dr. Russell, if our world is so little, and the universe is so great, can we really believe that God pays any attention to us human beings?

The noted astronomer answered, "That all depends, Madam, on how big a God you believe in."

The immense magnitude of the universe demands a bigger God than most of us know. Stretch your mind and soul on the stars, and you will make more room there for a greater God.

PART 7:
EYES ON THE FUTURE

41

But What Can You Expect?

A S I SIT IN MY STUDY NEAR THE WHISPERING
waters of Lake Charlevoix and ponder the abundant life
and death around me in tall, aspiring trees and in rotting logs,
and meditate on human worth, it seems impossible that once
upon a time there was no living thing here at Wide Sky Harbor.
Nothing whatever. No whirring wings of darting redstarts, king-
fishers, scarlet tanagers, and many-colored dragonflies, no perch
fry and fingerling bass along the shallow water's edge, no
rhythmic bending and bowing of wind-lulled birches, no white-
tailed deer daintily sipping from the waters that lave their feet.
Once there were no gently tossing waters to bathe the shores,
no rolling green hills that pull up purple shadow-quilts under
which they slumber at night, and no earth.

If once there was no earth at all, whence then all this beauty
and grandeur? People of faith everywhere believe that God
created the earth. How He did it, what techniques and processes He used, are causes of wide disagreement. The most
widely accepted scientific theory concerning the birth of this
planet is called the "tidal wave theory." It suggests that far in
the past, roughly five thousand million years ago, some great
star came close to a small star now known as "the sun." This
near collision produed a mighty wave of gases upon the sun.

145

The wave of flaming gases was pulled farther and farther out
from the sun by the gravitational tug of the on-going star until
at last the wave was wrenched away. But as the larger star re-
ceded into the distant heavens, its attraction for the wave of
fiery gases diminished, while the nearer sun's attraction remained strong. The disconnected strands of gases, part of the
broken wave, began whirling around the sun, tethered by the
force of gravity, and thus became our solar system of parent sun
and planet offspring. The theory declares that the gases con-
densed first into thicker gaseous matter, then into liquid, and
still later into rock. Then followed atmosphere and water made
up of molecules drawn from the vast spaces beyond the earth,
and finally, after countless millions of years, all the budding
and blooming, swimming, crawling, walking and flying things
of earth we call life.

Science says that this is what apparently happened: earth
became the rocky offspring of the distant flaming sun. (And
science, with the help of the spectroscope, shows that elements
of the earth are the same as those on the sun, just as a torn
piece of dress goods may give evidence of belonging to the
material and pattern of the original garment.) Faith says if

earth originally came from the sun, it did not happen accidentally. God did it. It was His planning, His method of creating,
by making first a sun and then smaller celestial bodies from the
larger. It is all His handiwork. Science and religion do not
conflict here. They but complement each other. Science cleaves
to its own activity . . . analysis of process. Religion holds to
its specialty of worth. Science shows us what has been done in
nature, and religion claims that what has been done is God's
doing, and it is good. Science discovers facts. Religion places a
value upon them and interprets them in the light of what one
believes about God and His purposes.

The best evidence we have of what God may do with this
world and with us is found in what God has already done
with the world and with us. This is why religious faith is both
retrospective and expectant, both historical and hopeful. Faith
looks backward and selects events that are good and meaningful and declares, "God did it" and then looks forward to the
good that ought to be and proclaims, "God can do it, because He has already done something just as good and just as
great." The history of the Hebrew people is rife with remarkable events which parents recited to their children, incidents
showing what man could expect of God. The Almighty had led
the children of Israel out of bondage to the Egyptians: that
kind of deliverance could be expected of God. The people were
given a place in a Promised Land of rich fields and great herds
of cattle and flocks of sheep. Such good fortune did not
happen accidentally. It was God's doing and emblematic of
what man could hope for from God.

The cynical are constantly repeating, when trouble comes,
when human nature shows its flaws, when picnic plans are
spoiled by rain, "But what can you expect?" Well, what *can*
we expect in this kind of world? For one thing, based on the
best evidence we have, we can expect all the rampant earthly
glory we shall ever know in nature to arise out of the ashes of
a burnt-out mass of spinning gases. We can expect that sort of
thing from God. And if that is not "too good to be true" then
nothing is. This is what *has* happened under God. It is the

147

sort of thing we can expect Him to do, the seemingly impossible, bringing order out of chaos and beauty out of ashes.

That is a faith I'm holding to in these turbulent days.

Care to join me?

42

On Reaching the Goal

NIGHT BEFORE LAST OUR REGION SUFFERED A heavy wind-and-rain storm. Great gusts of wind blew fitfully, angrily, bending the trees that line our trail, rattling our doors, fiercely pelting our windows with giant raindrops. The next day when I visited our family's woodland retreat I came upon a fledgling bird lying dead below its nest. Perhaps the fall from the nest injured it and the cold rain finished it. It was well feathered out, this baby phoebe, and about ready to fly if it had been spared. Plump it was, too, from many a rich meal of insects and worms. But its brief life was already spent before its talent for flying could be tested. The mother bird had invested weeks incubating the eggs and warming and feeding that birdling. All that care and nurture, and nothing would come of it now. That nestling was meant to stroke the sky with wind-loving wings, but now it would never know the meaning of flight. The fledgling had missed the mark of becoming a bird.

Several years ago, while on a walk through the woods in the springtime, I came upon a stillborn whitetail deer fawn. The bottoms of its hoofs were clean; it had never stood upon its feet. Through some unknown defect the fawn had been born breathless, and thus had missed fulfillment of its creaturehood. It was meant to be a dappled, elfin shadow among other shadows on the forest floor. Later it should have become a reddish-brown wood-spirit, bounding through grassy glades, frequenting hidden, nearly forgotten forest trails, browsing on shoots of birches, sipping from icy streams, mating and bearing its own young. But the fawn missed fulfillment. Its further development was blocked at birth.

Perhaps the pity we hold for the young that die is linked to our awareness that a lack of fulfillment is one of life's sorriest tragedies. In the death of young creatures there are tendencies that are thwarted before they reach their goals and capacities that are blocked and foiled forever.

But death is not the only way fulfillment of latent possibilities is frustrated. In human beings sin thwarts realization of life's highest goals. Indeed, this is one of the real meanings of moral evil; it is a failing, a blocking, or a misdirection of the good; a wrong aim; a missing of the mark. The word commonly translated "sin" in the New Testament is a Greek word used as a term in archery, and it means "to miss the mark." Any archer who aimed his arrow toward a target and missed it was quite literally a "sinner." The word was carried over from that graphic original meaning to broader applications and used to describe any disharmony with the purpose of God. To sin meant to use any part of our nature in such a way as to stray from God's intentions for us. If God wills good toward all of His children, then sin is anything that thwarts the good in any of us. It is anything that hinders an individual or the whole social order from achieving the good God desires.

Are not many of our worst troubles caused by some good arrows that go astray and maim or destroy someone's life, often our own? The old Roman proverb, "Optima corrupta pessima" expressed a deep insight — "The best things when corrupted become the worst." Of course they do. See, for instance, how a commendable service motive becomes self-service. Many young graduates of schools of business believe their career to be a vocation, a calling to answer some human need. Of course they hope to make money, but they aim to put service first and money second. But soon, for many of them, the ambition to make money at any cost begins to stir within them. The early high ideals become easily corrupted. First, with a twinge of conscience, a young businessman tolerates practices which seem only slightly shady. Then he may engage in exploitation of the public through unfair prices, small misrepresentations, a little adulteration of his product, a limited amount of misbranding. Bottles that look very large and hold very little, dummy bottoms in boxes, carelessly constructed buildings, advertisements that claim too much for products sold, these are

150

only a few of the ways people let business principles miss the mark.

Sex easily goes astray. Young people are too often told they should not indulge in sex relations because sex is unclean and ugly. The very opposite is true; the unmarried should not indulge because sex is a good and beautiful thing reserved for those who are wholly, unreservedly committed to each other in marriage, and thus the relationship of sex is sacramental, having holy meanings. To use it outside of marriage is to profane a holy thing.

While the Victorians of a few generations past perverted the idea of sex by treating it as nasty, the present generation has debased and corrupted the meaning of sex by making a gimmick of it, trifling with it. We have used sex appeal as a sort of carrot to hang before people to lead them to buy toothpaste, tobacco, automobiles, and almost every kind of gadget on the market. Moreover, we have made "sex" a synonym of irresponsibility, of promiscuity and debauchery, and then have labeled this wild confusion "love." But these things are not love and have nothing to do with unselfish love or with lasting happiness.

Our problem is not how to handle the bad thing, sex, but how to preserve the good thing from waywardness, how to make it reach its goal of being sacramental, expressing the good in human nature. Any other use of this function is sin, in the sense of "missing the mark."

Religion, too, often misses its goal. While the function of religion is to remind us of the God who is always near us and to prompt us to use His power and to obey His will, religion often goes astray. Religion can be misdirected so that it becomes a retreat from the real world, from life's ugly facts, a search for mental comfort and spiritual ease. Such religion becomes a substitute for intelligent thought, and it takes the place of an agonizing involvement in the woes of one's fellow men.

Some people find that contemplating God is so satisfying that they become indifferent to the hurts of human beings around them. Some use the faith that was meant to be armor

to protect them in life's struggles as a cloak to hide their real faults. Others use religion like a spare tire — only in emergencies.

Religion can shrink the mind or stretch it; it can make one

narrowly bigoted or bigger and more understanding of others; it can confirm one's prejudices or expand one's compassions. Indeed, religion's most popular feature is its flexibility: it can be adapted to whatever we wish to do. But such a limp religion is like a flimsy arrow, sure to miss its target. And a religion that doesn't serve its high purpose is sin.

All the way from a dead nestling bird and a stillborn fawn through business deals, sex, and religion, tragedy is found in lack of fulfillment, missing the goal. Life's great glory is in fulfillment, hitting the target, being what God means us to be, doing what God wants us to do.

43

The Sense of Things Beyond

O NE FASCINATION FOUND IN TRAMPING through woods and fields lies in the surprise always awaiting the wanderer just a step beyond. The world looks unexciting and commonplace. Then the unexpected happens, and an uneventful day becomes memorable. Not long ago two friends of ours, Oscar and Isabell, tramped with our little family along a narrow, shadowy forest path in Wildwood, their Northland resort acreage. We had precious little time together, so our walking was to the tune of loud chatter as we caught up on the latest news of mutual friends and made plans for the future. The excited and clamorous talk, the pounding of ten feet upon the forest path, and the cracking of brush as we swept clutching limbs from before our faces forewarned all denizens of the woods of our coming. Because of our noisiness, we expected to see nothing but trees and shrubs, ferns and mushrooms, and other things rooted to the earth and unable to escape us. The forest appeared utterly empty of flying or running creatures. Then past our heads, so close we had to dodge its pounding wings, there rocketed a ruffed grouse. We could almost smell his feather dust and see the flickering sparkle of excitement in his eyes. As we watched him wing his twisting, turning way down the cramped forest aisles, we wondered aloud at his waiting there, beyond us, until we almost stepped upon him. It was as if he *meant* to surprise us by fairly exploding in our faces.

The brook banks may look deserted of life. But another step sends a leopard frog catapulting over the grasses into the amber waters. The brook itself often appears to be empty of all else but water, stones, and vegetation. Then a mighty swirl stirs up the silt beneath a log and a trim, jewel-marked brook trout dashes upstream to its den beneath the cedar roots. I've glanced up a trail when all was still and have seen a mink star-

ing back at me. A few days ago I stepped out from behind a
large poplar tree near our cabin, intending only to take a look
at the meadow, and saw a huge doe strolling along within but
a few yards of where I stood. She was walking upwind of me,
unhurried and enjoying the late afternoon sunshine. I've knocked
off my hat on a low-hanging apple tree limb and reached to get
it, only to have the action interrupted by the piercing stare of a

raccoon who has halted his digging for grubs under decaying brush to give me an irritated "once-over." Always, to the observer, a nature ramble is a venturesome experience. Just beyond where you are, perhaps before you finish taking your next step, the unexpected will happen.

Few tragedies can occur to the human spirit so deadly in effect as the loss of a consciousness of good things just ahead. It makes for boredom and a feeling of uselessness. In 1838 a worker in the United States Patent Office quit his position, declaring in his letter of resignation, which is still on file in the Hall of Archives in Washington, "There is no future in the Patent Office; all the great inventions have been accomplished." A year later daguerreotype was invented, ushering in the age of photography. There followed the invention of the telephone, the jet-propulsion engine, diesel engine, motion pictures, victrolas, radio, submarines, automobiles, airships, the development of life-saving insulin, sulfa drugs, penicillin, and new surgical techniques. Atomic power has become usable and, we hope, controllable. Poor fellow — "all the great inventions have been accomplished." He's dead, even if he still breathes.

Even religious people sometimes suffer from a lack of cheerful expectancy. If they look forward at all, it is toward calamity, as if this were not our Father's world, but wholly in the hands of a malevolent fate. Some anonymous poet has poked wholesome fun at these mourners:

> My grandad, viewing earth's worn cogs,
> Said things were going to the dogs;
> His grandad, in his house of logs,
> Said things are going to the dogs;
> His grandad, in his old skin togs,
> Said things are going to the dogs.
> There's one thing that I have to state —
> The dogs have had a good long wait.

This is not to overlook the serious crisis our world faces, with its struggle between materialism and spiritual forces, between totalitarian governments and democracies, between

156

Christ and antichrist. Faith never blinds a person to things as they are. However, faith does insist that, besides the awful present and the disturbing past, the future must be counted in before the whole story can be told concerning the fate of the world or the fate of a person. And just beyond the present, perhaps no more than a step ahead, lies God's wondrous surprise.

The people without a sense of good things just beyond are the ones who mutiny and chain Columbus to the deck of his ship because they have sailed too long without sight of land and are sure the voyage is hopeless. They are the wailers who early begin to mourn the loss of a Revolutionary War and beg Washington to surrender at Boston. They are the disciples who see their Lord crucified and with a shrug of the shoulders say, "Let's go back to our fishing!" They have no sense of the good that might lie just beyond — a new continent, or a victory, or a resurrection.

Faith is that hopeful spirit that looks upon the world, upon human nature, and even upon trouble with a spirit of anticipation akin to the expectancy with which one starts a tramp down a woodland trail. "I wonder what surprise lies just ahead," we say to ourselves. "I wonder what great good will come out of this."

From the time we first look upon our newborn child to the day we tenderly lay a loved one away in final rest, much of the wonder and glory of life abides in an awareness that "This is not all. There is more ahead."

About the Author

Harold Kohn's varied interests — in religion, psychology and philosophy, in nature and art — have found expression in a many-faceted career. Dr. Kohn is a clergyman (most recently the minister of the First Congregational Church, Charlevoix, Michigan for twelve years, and now retired because of decline in health); a counsellor of the troubled; a writer on nature, psychology and inspirational subjects; the author of seven books (six of which have been book club selections), which he has also illustrated with line drawings; the writer of a nationally syndicated column "Lift for Living" and many magazine articles, which have appeared in such publications as *The Christian Herald, Church and Home,* and *The Reader's Digest.* Selections from his writings appear in anthologies of the world's wisdom and inspiration.

Dr. Kohn is a lecturer in great demand at colleges and conventions. In 1963 he was presented "The Michigan Citizenship Award" by Governor George Romney, having been selected as one of ten citizens who had given "distinguished leadership to the people of Michigan" in the preceding ten-year period. Dr. Kohn was the only clergyman to be chosen for this high honor. Another recent recognition was the honorary degree of Doctor of Humane Letters bestowed upon him by Olivet College.

His B. A. degree is from North Central College of Naperville, Illinois and graduate work was taken at Evangelical Theological Seminary.

Dr. Kohn and his wife Marian live at Hidden Brook, in the middle of a forty-acre plot of birch, evergreen, maple and beech forest, trout stream and ponds, close to Lake Charlevoix, not far from Lake Michigan, and about five miles from the city of "Charlevoix the Beautiful" — in the clean air which his uncertain health requires, and amidst the natural surroundings he loves. This haven is often visited by the Kohns' daughter and son-in-law, Carolyn and Larry Minch, grandsons Timmy and Kevin, and hosts of readers eager to meet the author and to see Hidden Brook.

159